Treat Me Like Your Car

A Man's Guide to Treating a Lady

Pilar Lastra

iUniverse, Inc.
Bloomington

Treat Me Like Your Car
A Man's Guide to Treating a Lady

iUniverse books may be ordered through booksellers or by contacting:

iUniverse
1663 Liberty Drive
Bloomington, IN 47403
www.iuniverse.com
1-800-Authors (1-800-288-4677)

Special edit thanks to Cara Bedick and Jay Jay Nesheim

ISBN: 978-1-4620-4220-3 (sc)
ISBN: 978-1-4620-4219-7 (hc)
ISBN: 978-1-4620-4555-6 (e)

Library of Congress Control Number: 2011913681

Printed in the United States of America

iUniverse rev. date: 09/27/2011

Contents

Author's Note

Have you ever wondered why women don't come with instruction manuals?

Sometimes I wish we were born with one. I will be the first to admit that I am one of the many women who have said, "I wish he'd understand me," or "I wish he'd treat me better, be a little more considerate, rekindle the romance ..." and a whole slew of other requests. Does any of this sound familiar to you? If you are a man reading this and thinking, *I do everything she wants me to but it just isn't enough*, well then, cool your jets, Dexter, the manual is here!

By reading this book, your efforts won't go unnoticed. Even if your girlfriend bought it for you because she was tired of complaining about you just not "getting it," or if you bought it for yourself because you are tired of every woman nagging you about the same thing, any man who tries just a little harder to understand what a woman wants should be applauded.

You're about to learn just how to get on a woman's good side, and I promise, it will keep you from sleeping on the couch and will make both of your lives easier. The manual is right here, in your hands.

Introduction

When I decided to move from San Antonio to Los Angeles, I was broke, with only a beat-up 1990 Mustang to my name. I remember taking my car to the mechanic to get it checked out before hitting the road; he took one look under the hood, slammed it down, and said, "You won't get halfway to El Paso." My radiator was cracked, my hoses needed to be replaced, my transmission was slipping, and that was just the start; it was quickly obvious that getting my car fixed by a professional was financially out of the question. But fixing the car myself with the help of a fifteen-dollar Haynes repair manual and junkyard parts was a great alternative.

Rebuilding my car taught me how to make friends at the junkyard, but it also taught me that everything functions for a reason—if you neglect one part of your car, it can lead to problems in other areas. And fixing one part to get by but not finding the root of the problem can cause a serious dilemma at an inconvenient time—like the time I changed all of the belts but forgot to test the alternator. This made for an unexpected pit-stop in the middle of the blazing hot Arizona desert on my quest to Los Angeles.

When I finally made it to Los Angeles, I found dating to be frustrating. Acts of chivalry had been as common in my hometown of San Antonio, Texas, as palm trees were in my new home. However, in LA, a man wouldn't even open a car door for a woman. I started to observe men and their behavior, and the first thing I realized was that they all displayed respect and love for their cars. They never missed a tune-up date; they cleaned and polished frequently; they insured their tires; and they even went as far as parking a block away to avoid a door ding. Cars were a universal language all men spoke and understood.

At the same time, whether I was chatting with my listeners on Playboy Radio (where I gave relationship advice on love, sex, and travel through the eyes of a Playmate), or listening to women I worked with on the TV show *Deal or No Deal,* or talking to my fellow Playmate sisters about how their men just didn't "get it," I began to realize that there were a number of common problems that all relationships face.

My knowledge and passion for cars expanded when I became the host of my car-culture show called *Hot Laps* on Playboy.com, and then Mazda helped start my racing career. Having worked on a car also gave me an advantage, as I was able to translate relationship needs and frustrations into a language everyone could understand: cars.

Applying my theory started working in problem areas in my own love life, and soon I started offering friends and listeners a good alternative to communication in their own relationships. Learning how to work on a car, combined with my own unforgettable dating experiences and the experiences and problems my friends faced in their relationships, inspired me to write *Treat Me Like Your Car: A Man's Guide to Treating a Lady.*

I'm here to tell you that it's a lot easier than everyone's been making it out to be. What women want is simple. Simple enough, in fact, to explain in just five words:

Treat me like your car.

Why "treat me like your car" and not "treat me like a princess," a common phrase used to explain how women should and would like to be treated? It's not our fault; we spent our most impressionable years watching fairytales that all had the same ending: Prince Charming riding in on a white horse and saving the maiden—maybe with a perfect kiss, maybe by climbing a tower or slaughtering a dragon, but regardless of how, he knew what to do.

This is why we think every man should just instinctively know what we, as women, want and need. In the midst of the arguments fighting over what she wants, you have most likely heard these infamous words: "All I ask is that you treat me like a princess!" In our eyes, we aren't asking for much. Cinderella never had to spell it out for her man. When you hear the word "princess," what do you think of? Maybe a tiara, crown jewels, or a castle? Men tend to take the literal sense of the word. But women, we say "treat me like a princess" and think of honor, kindness, loyalty, and respect. We want to be valued as if we were truly princesses.

There's the first problem—men and women think in different languages. Now when it comes to your car, you know that if you want your baby to run smoothly, you have to at least keep up with the minimum-scheduled maintenance. Check the oil every so often, inspect the tires for pressure and wear, get them rotated if they need it, lubricate the locks, and keep up your dates with the car wash. And if you really want to take care of it, have the proper rags and tools on hand to clean off any sudden dirt or fingerprints.

Shoot, after all a man does for his car, screw the princess crap, we want you to treat us like your car!

Out of all the men I have met—and between my duties as a model on *Deal or No Deal* and as a Playmate hosting many Playboy parties, that's a lot—four out of five men treat their cars better than they do their women. (Maybe it's because cars don't talk back?) Regardless of why, it's what men do, and in the same way men are confused by the phrase "treat me like a princess," there are many women out there yearning to scream at their men, "It's just a car!" Women everywhere have been lectured about using the door handle that has been strategically placed to open and close the car door as to not leave fingerprints on the window. Yet a man will leave dishes in the sink for his girlfriend to clean up when there is a dishwasher strategically placed next to it. Women have seen their men stress out if they hear an unusual rattle in their engines, stopping to try and figure it out, maybe even pulling right into a garage. But what about their girlfriends' cries for attention that go unnoticed?

Think of me as the ultimate translator. As a woman, I'm fluent in the language of princesses, but after years of working on cars and speaking with many different types of men, I also speak "hot rod." *Treat Me Like Your Car* will help make treating your woman like a lady as easy as taking care of your car. Romance isn't dead, it just needs a jump start.

Chapter 1:

Pit Stop

When you're in the market for a car, you usually have a mental checklist of what you're looking for and what you can afford. Knowing these things when you begin shopping around will save you and the salesperson some time. For instance, you're probably not going to walk into a Maserati dealership when you know that the payment you are willing and able to make is for a Ford.

Now there's nothing wrong with checking out what's available at the exotic dealership, as long as you inform the salesperson you are not exactly in the market to buy at the time—you're just having fun checking out the display. This will also keep the salesperson from slashing your tires after you have made him or her take you on an entire day of test drives and prep five hot dogs for you just to hear you say at the end of the day, "Well, hey, thanks a bunch, I was just looking." The salesperson could have spent his or her time with a potential buyer who was actually looking to seal the deal.

A good friend of mine in the car industry calls people like this "looky-loos," people who like to just look and waste your time. He truly doesn't mind them and can have a lot of fun showing them fast cars just as long as they tell him their intentions up front. Now, while a woman's reaction to a "looky-loo" in dating may differ slightly, dating, in general, isn't any different. This time you're in the market for a relationship. And as you'll see throughout the course of this book, the two are a lot more similar than you would think.

Similar to the questions you would ask yourself to save some time while looking to buy a car, there's a mental checklist to go through as you try to find the right girl that, in this case, will save everyone time, headaches, and heartaches. Women, like cars, can be found in so many different places, shapes, sizes, and budgets, with all sorts of bells and whistles. Beginning your search can become extremely overwhelming very quickly, so the first thing we're going to do is try to narrow things down a bit and figure out what you are looking for.

So what are you in the market for? Something long term that you would like to buy, a short-term lease, or just a test drive? Knowing you are just looking to have fun and go on a couple of test drives is fine, just as long as you are honest with the salesperson. The same goes for dating. Telling a girl you are not at a place in your life to make any big decisions right now is okay. There is never anything wrong with honesty; this allows the girl to make the choice if she wants to stick around for the fun or if she would rather try to invest her time in something that might look a little more promising. Don't worry; there are plenty of girls out there who are not always looking to be in a relationship.

KNOW YOUR BUDGET

If you're not sure what you're looking for, the first thing to do is *know your budget*. The same way you consider what you can financially afford each month on a car payment, you should consider what you can emotionally afford to give to a relationship.

Some women are higher-maintenance emotionally than others, and some women just want to date and not even think of marriage or monogamy.

On the flipside, there are girls who know they are not just looking to casually date. Did you know there are some cars you cannot even test drive without being a serious buyer? Take a $1.7 million Bugatti Veyron. This car is classy, sleek, and elegant, and at 137 mph, the nose of the car is automatically lowered two inches and the rear spoiler slides into slipstream. This two-million-dollar baby takes you from zero to sixty mph in 2.4 seconds. Even more impressively, the Bugatti takes you from zero to sixty and back to zero in less than five seconds. Zero to 180 mph in fourteen seconds. With a top speed of 253 mph, you won't get close enough to take a picture of this car if you are not a serious buyer, and the salesperson will have no problem telling you that up front. There is no leasing option on this bad girl. You either enter the dealership with the intention of buying this beauty and taking her home to meet the family or you're not getting anywhere near it.

Some lots know exactly what they are looking for—a serious buyer who can afford this kind of car and its thirty-thousand-dollar tires. And some women know they are looking for someone who can handle a serious relationship and would not even date a man who is emotionally unavailable.

So take the time to first figure out what you are looking for, and when you know, be honest about it. Don't tell a girl you are looking for a long-term commitment when you know your budget can only afford a short-term lease. Honesty will make everything run a bit more smoothly.

PUT YOUR PEDAL TO THE METAL

Just telling a girl you're not looking for a relationship right now isn't always enough. Your actions speak louder than words. If you continue to court her and sleep with her regularly, eventually she is going to think all you needed was time, and not for one second will she think that you meant you didn't want to be monogamous. Be clear on your meaning about what you are looking for. Having a slightly uncomfortable conversation early on, or cutting yourself off early if you think she is getting the wrong impression, is a lot easier than dealing with stronger consequences down the road.

*   *   *

Knowing what you are looking for before you step into the dealership isn't just for the other party's benefit. Imagine entering a dealership planning to walk off the lot with a car that is going to run you five hundred dollars a month. This is a payment you know you can comfortably afford; maybe you're looking at a stock Cadillac CTS. But the salesperson convinces you that if you just put another thousand dollars down, and for only a measly extra one hundred seventy-five bucks a month you can walk off the lot with a brand new Cadillac Escalade with twenty-two-inch rims and a five-thousand-dollar rebate, and he can even get you a 1.9 percent interest rate on all new cars in stock. So your brain starts working and you quickly start to think, *Well, if I cut back on beer and start eating at home a little more, really, what's an extra one hundred seventy-five bucks a month? And with the rebate, I'm getting a steal!*

The salesman has convinced you to go for it—something you didn't want in the first place. At first you are happy with your great deal, but then at your first fill-up you realize gas prices are outrageous. A few months in, you realize the difference between replacing a blown-out twenty-inch tire and a twenty-two-inch tire is almost your new monthly car payment, and ultimately you realize how much it sucks to feel trapped in something you really didn't want to begin with.

Had you known exactly what you were looking for when you walked onto that lot, no one could have persuaded you to buy anything you weren't really comfortable with. I have seen it happen too many times, where a guy who isn't ready to be in a serious relationship starts dating a great girl who knows what she wants—to get engaged—and the guy commits to it. But before you know it, all he does is complain and cry about not being happy and how he is missing the single life—so much so that he ends up picking random fights just to ruin the relationship so he can get out of a situation he never meant to be in.

Guys and girls sometimes bite off more than they can emotionally afford to chew and end up suffering for their decisions in the long run. So take the time to know what you want, and don't take on more than you can handle emotionally or financially. You can always commit to a lease with an option to buy if you change your mind later on down the road and decide that you are ready for a serious commitment.

YOUR SEARCH BEGINS WITH A CARFAX REPORT

Let's slip into an automobile fantasy, shall we? So you are minding your business driving to work one day, and suddenly, from out of the heavens above, you see her. Irresistible and breathtaking, straight from any man's dream, she stops you right in your tracks, with a body you long to wax and an engine you can't wait to rev. This cherry-red 1967 Ford Mustang Shelby GT500 with black racing stripes has got wheels you'd love to see spin for days. You end up shelling out your life savings to get your hands on this beauty. Just like that! You weren't even in the market to buy a car, and you found it, the perfect "Eleanor," the car of your dreams.

This also happens to be exactly how most people end up in a relationship when they aren't even looking for one. The last thing you needed in life was to have to put up with pleasing a woman.

You had everything going for you—all you wanted to do was focus on your career and hang out with the guys. But no, you just couldn't resist, you had to ask her out, didn't you? Dating is great, and for the first couple of months you are in complete bliss. You can't get enough of each other. It's after you really get to know the person that you start to have problems.

Let's go back to our automobile fantasy, when you first bought the Shelby GT500. You were so in love you took that car everywhere, and your friends would tell you what a great car you had. And you might have said she's a gas guzzler, but she sure is worth every bit of it.

Then suddenly you are driving back from one of those great nights out and you hear an unfamiliar noise. At first you don't pay too much attention, but then you realize you're starting to smell a peculiar odor coming from the vents. Before you know it, you are going crazy troubleshooting the stupid car, trying to figure out what went wrong, what special attention it needs—and even more taxing and time-consuming, you obsess over all of its previous issues. What should you do? Get rid of it before it becomes a money pit, or ride it out for a while and hope you don't have to file a Chapter 7 after paying for the repairs? You thought she was perfect. She was in mint condition, not a single dent in her body.

A detailed car-history report explains that your precious Shelby GT500 was in a disastrous head-on collision with her previous owner at the helm. Too bad he forgot to mention that before he took your $150,000 life savings! Just like that. In less time than the seven seconds your Shelby GT500 is supposed to get you from zero to sixty, your perfect "Eleanor" became a depressing "Igor."

Sound familiar? Sure it does; every relationship is smooth and easy in the beginning. It's when both of your true colors start to show that more of the truth comes out, and you may begin to have second thoughts. We all have a past of some sort, and some women may not want to volunteer the information up front. Some just don't care and will tell you about every guy they have ever dated/married/had kids with/divorced. Some, through their behavior, will tell you whether they have been in a rough relationship before. Some women will make it easy for you, and some will make you do your homework to find out their dating history and what special attention they need. (And everyone needs some, in one area or another.)

TALES FROM THE ROAD

I once dated a guy who was very religious. We hit it off so well, we were always laughing and really enjoyed each other's company; we even went to church together every Sunday. When we first met, he asked me what I did for a living. I knew he was very religious, so I told him I did promotional modeling. It wasn't a lie—I did do promotional modeling—but I left out the name of the company I worked for, and he never asked. I didn't think it would come up again.

About three months later, one of his ex-girlfriends was playing snoop-dog and found out that I was a Playboy Playmate. Not only did she tell him, she told his entire family! This was so not cool! I would have been better off just telling him I was a Playmate from the beginning so he could have made a choice whether to deal with it and move forward with our relationship or end it. I felt like those CarFax commercials, where you see a car in flames being extinguished by the firefighters, and on the screen you see someone typing the classified ad for the car that says something along the lines of, "1998 Mustang, runs great, minor smoke damage." But then he deletes that and replaces the words "minor smoke damage" with "this car is hot." He isn't lying—but he isn't telling the whole truth.

I can't believe I am about to admit this, because I promised myself I would never be that woman who thinks she can change a man or his beliefs, but I figured if I just gave our relationship some time, he would get to know me for who I was and not judge me based on my past. I thought he would proceed to fall so deeply in love with me that it wouldn't matter whether or not I was a Playmate. Unfortunately, it didn't work out that way. He flipped when he found out, because he felt betrayed that I didn't tell him three months prior when he had asked me what I did for a living. Batting my eyelashes wasn't going to get me out of this mess. We continued to date, but we didn't last much longer. He developed trust issues that affected many of his future relationships, and I can't blame him.

*   *   *

It's extremely important to take your time to get to know someone before you get serious with her. Guys and girls have issues with insecurities, image, jealousy, trust, abandonment, commitment, religion, communication, birth control—the list goes on—and all of these can end up being serious problems further down the road.

I have a great friend who dated a girl for three years and was completely monogamous the entire time. However, because her previous boyfriend strayed so many times, she was always accusing my friend of cheating on her. She was so convinced he was cheating that she went out and slept with a mutual acquaintance just to get back at him. When he found out, he was so hurt that he ended the relationship and now will not commit to anyone because of the pain his last girlfriend caused him. He thinks it is a waste of time to commit to a girl when no matter what you do or don't do, she is still going to accuse you of cheating.

Do you see the vicious cycle here? My ex-boyfriend now has trust issues with his new girlfriend because of the fact that I was not completely honest with him. It's not her fault, but she is the one who has to deal with constant questions because of one bad relationship in his past. He ended up explaining to her the reason why we broke up, and as dumb and unfair as it is that he is holding her accountable for my mistake, at least she now understands why he questions every answer she gives him.

If you take the time to find out why a woman is single or why she broke up with her last boyfriend, you will learn a lot. I went on a couple of dates with a guy, and he asked me why I left my previous relationship. I told him I wanted kids and the other person did not. Then my date asked if I wanted kids soon. I said sooner than later, and after that first date, he told me we weren't really meant for each other. We were both up front about what we wanted and realized we were better off as friends. Even if either of us were the tiniest bit annoyed or disappointed at the moment, it sure beat finding the same information out a couple of years into the relationship, when I would have started pushing for kids.

In the beginning of a relationship, girls and guys always play the "cool card." They act like nothing bugs them, that they are the perfect mates, and that each can still have ultimate freedom. Then a couple months down the road, your phone won't stop blowing up when you're out with the guys because she wants to know if you really are where you say you are. It would have made your life a lot easier had you known her last boyfriend used to tell her he was going to hang out for guys' night when he was really on a date with his *other* girlfriend—hence her blowing up your phone.

So how does that CarFax commercial end again? Oh yeah. Never buy a car without a car-history report. The same applies to relationships. Never get serious without knowing a person's past. I'm not telling you to judge a person on her past. The past is the past and you are in her present, but at least this way you will know what you're dealing with before you really have to deal with it. Ultimately, if you pull a car-history report before you buy the car and you know that you are going to have to spend some time and money on it for repairs, that's okay, because now you know what you are getting yourself into.

A COLT WILL NEVER BE A MUSTANG

"In a world where you can be anything, be yourself." I read this quote somewhere by Etta Turner, and it has stuck with me ever since. Being yourself is the only way to be. There is someone out there who will adore you for who you are and not for someone you are trying to be. If you have a Dodge Colt, no matter what you do to modify it, it will never be a Ford Mustang. Why? Because even though you may think they both have horse characteristics, they have two different manufacturers, and that's just the beginning of their differences. If you are a Pinto, be a Pinto. The last thing you want to do is pretend you are a Lamborghini. Don't even try to pretend you can octane boost yourself into being able to keep up with a Lamborghini for a second. You can't, not even with the best upgrades, and you will blow your engine trying. And that is okay, because someone will buy a Pinto and love it just the way it is.

TALES FROM THE ROAD

I will never forget my first car. It was a baby-blue 1989 Dodge Colt. Who would have ever thought that out of all the cars at the dealership, I was going to end up bringing home the Dodge Colt?

To this day, my old high school friends make fun of me and bring up stories about that car. And also to this day, I can tell you every amazing and unique quality about that car, such as the little lever on the bottom left-hand side of the driver's seat that would raise and lower the height of the seat. I knew exactly what I was getting into every time I got in that car.

It wasn't a baby-blue Dodge Colt that had some after-market upgrades so people would think it was some kind of a pimp ride. It didn't have a loud, obnoxious stereo system that caught everyone's attention when I was pulling up. It didn't have spinners on the rims—heck, I didn't even have rims on that puppy, I had hubcaps. It was what it was, never pretending to be anything it wasn't. My friends may have laughed at it, but my Colt was perfect for me.

It is the same way I fall in love with a guy who can be himself. For some reason, when a guy first meets a girl he puts on a show—girls do it too, I know—but we are not in algebra, boys; two negatives don't make a positive. And there's a difference between being on your best behavior and trying to appear as though you are perfect. Let a girl get to know who you are—not your representative or who you wish you were—from the very beginning.

*   *   *

I went through a similar phase when I bought my second car. It was a red 1990 Ford Mustang. Man, I really loved that car! It made me feel cool. I went crazy with the after-market upgrades; I put ghetto-fabulous, chrome Tri-Star wheels on it, bought an amazing stereo system with a fifteen-inch subwoofer in my trunk, and had a really cool clear-top amplifier. I had no idea what it did but it just looked cool. To top it off, I shelled out some serious cash so my sister's high school sweetheart could throw on a new paint job. I thought I was so cool rolling around in my pimped-out ride. The paint job was crappy and had the texture of an orange peel, but it was shiny and new! I looked like an idiot in it but felt awesome! I would leave my window rolled down so I could climb in through it, because I was too cool to open the door.

Thankfully, this phase only lasted a summer. Very shortly after, I was missing my sweet Dodge Colt. I soon went back to putting stock rims on the Mustang and removing the amp and the subwoofer and special front speakers. I realized it was a regular Mustang—not a Mustang GT, just a Mustang. I wanted that car to look like it had a 5.0 engine in it, but it really only had a 2.3 liter. And even if I would have tried to upgrade the engine to a 5.0 (which I looked into, trust me), it was impossible to get it to fit under the hood. There just wasn't enough room. I even tried to make it look like it had a dual exhaust by replacing the stock tailpipe with a larger chrome tailpipe that looked like a Flowmaster and adding in a dummy tailpipe on the right side— until one day when I backed into a curb and it fell off. I wanted people to believe my Mustang had 215 horsepower, but really, it only had 88. When I sold the car, I put all the accessories in the trunk and let the buyer take all the bells and whistles away.

Saying you love romantic walks on the beach to get someone to pay attention to you when the truth is you think it's overrated or you hate the smell of the ocean is like adding all those upgrades to the Mustang: pointless to begin with, and sooner or later that dummy tailpipe is going to fall off. If you think you're a dork, be a dork. If a girl doesn't want you for who you really are, that is not a girl you should be around anyway. This is all obvious stuff, but unfortunately, dating often includes a bit of bait and switch; like when you say you like my cat but you are really allergic to him. Or when you tell me you love to give back rubs but an entire year goes by without your offering one to me.

We can say "what you see is what you get," but the truth is, that first month of dating is a pony show. When you first start dating a person you are not dating the real him or her, you are dating who he or she wishes they were. I'm not pointing fingers here; I'm guilty of this too. When I have a clean slate, I want to be the perfect girlfriend, and I even want his friends to think I am perfect for him. It's like when you are filling out the "About you" section of an Internet dating site. My friends write that they are open and honest, compassionate, loving, caring, considerate, enjoy bike rides, and philosophy—when the truth is, yes, they are honest, compassionate, loving, caring and considerate—but on rare occasions and only for short periods of time. They would love to be all these great qualities all the time and might even have made attempts to be this perfect more often, just like that goal to learn how to ride that mountain bike bought a year ago and never used. And as far as philosophy goes, I love Philosophy too—"Philosophy" being a line of great beauty products sold at any upscale department store.

The bottom line is: false advertisements stink. So when you first start to date, please be who *you* are. Women hate it when a guy puts on an act to pretend he is Mr. Perfect, being so attentive in the beginning and then three months later, the romance is over. And all we have left are the memories of what you once were. We really do hold on to that. And we will want to hold you accountable for being what you made yourself out to be. That is why you will hear us say, "You never do ___ anymore!" Or "Remember when you would always ___," and you can easily fill in the blanks with whatever helpful, sweet, or romantic thing you did in the beginning but stopped doing. It's like my old Mustang. Had I sold it with the dummy dual exhaust, the new owner would have expected to see exhaust come out of both tailpipes, not just one. But luckily it fell off before I sold it, so I didn't have to explain to the new owner why nothing would come out of the muffler on the right.

If you aren't a great listener, don't pretend to be one. If being attentive isn't a natural ability of yours, don't pretend you are. If you really love sports, don't pretend to hate them. If you don't care, don't pretend you do just to make us happy, because your true colors will come out. Don't bite off more than you can chew pretending to be someone you are not. You wouldn't buy a Hummer if you couldn't keep up with the gas bill for the entire time that you own that car, so impress your lady with an act you can perform naturally every time you are together, all the time.

MORE TALES FROM THE ROAD

It's hard to keep up with an image that isn't yours. Like I said before, I know from personal experience. When I initially met my first serious boyfriend, I was leasing apartments for a living. I remember having a conversation with him in the kitchen of a great two-bedroom about how easy it would be to cook in such a big and open kitchen. I was really only trying to sell him on the apartment, but then he asked if I could cook. I figured I could impress him and flirt a little, and I told him I was a natural chef. The truth was, when it came to cooking, the only "natural" thing about me was how easily I memorized the phone numbers for my favorite takeout places. So we started dating, and he obviously expected me to cook. The first couple of times he came over for dinner, I would go to the nearest Italian restaurant and buy amazing dishes, come home, throw it all into my pots and pans, and take the to-go containers to the dumpsters to discard the evidence.

A few dinner dates in, after I managed to "cook" chicken parmigiana, baked ziti, and eggplant rollatini without even seeming like I had been in front of a stove at all, let alone all day, he started questioning the authenticity of the taste of my "home-cooked" meals. So I convinced my aunt to cook me home-cooked meals, using my dishware, which I would just bring back to my house. This was exhausting, but it was working. One day I had to ask my aunt to actually come over and help me cook dinner at my place because I got off work late and there was no way I could clean my apartment and go over to her house to pick up the meal. So she came over to help me out again. My plan would have turned out perfectly once again if only my boyfriend had not thought it would be cute if he came over early to help me in the kitchen, only to find me vacuuming while my aunt was in the kitchen cooking everything herself. We were so busted—but to be honest, it was such a relief to get caught. I didn't know how much longer I could have convinced my aunt to keep helping me.

Soon after, he asked me to cook for him again—only this time he specifically requested that I cook a small dinner in front of him. So I made him a chicken Caesar salad and soup with garlic bread. The salad came from a bag and the chicken was from the lunchmeat aisle, so it was not only cooked but was cut into the perfect salad-sized strips. The soup was from a can, so I poured it into a pot and put it on a stove to heat it. The garlic bread was also premade—all I had to do was pop it into the oven. We both thought it was a successful attempt at an easy meal.

The smell of the garlic bread filled my kitchen, and we were both getting hungry. He started congratulating me on my new "cooking" skills, and then we both noticed that the yummy garlicky smell had turned into a burnt-toast kind of smell. Sure enough, I burnt the first loaf of garlic bread. I started to throw a fit about not only burning the bread but being afraid I was going to burn the soup when my boyfriend walked over to the stove and informed me there was no way I could burn the soup. I thought he was being sweet until he showed me that this was because I never even turned on the stove. One good thing came out of this—he bought me some cookbooks, but I cursed the day I lied about being able to cook.

*   *   *

I understand that everyone wants to start off on the right foot, but how do you feel when you first date a girl and she pretends to be really easygoing and even says she loves sports, but after three months into your relationship she gets irritable about you always wanting to watch sports? It sucks to feel deceived, and even worse, the characteristics that made you feel compatible in the first place have vanished. Trying to be someone you're not is trouble from the start, like my pimped-out 1990 Mustang. It looked better with all the stock parts. We want to date the man you really are from the beginning.

My friend Tamika, a girl I worked with on *Deal or No Deal,* had the perfect slogan for people who portray themselves to be something they are not: STP. Naturally I thought she was talking about the engine oil, but she informed me it means Something To Prove. I had a friend who would tell me and everyone he met that he was part owner of a development company and would constantly invite people to spend time at his developments with him and his "partners." We all bought it; he had the lie down to perfection, until one day one of his "partners" was explaining to me how they operated and what the responsibilities were of each owner. When I asked him about the role our mutual friend played in the company he said, "He does sales in one of our properties." This poor guy had made himself look like the biggest liar on Earth because he felt he had something to prove. Unfortunately for him, he didn't realize no one cared what he did for a living, we just enjoyed his company. But when we found out about his lying habit, it pretty much ended the friendships.

So the next time you meet someone and feel like it would be a good idea to act as though you have something to prove, remember that your dummy tailpipe is bound to fall off. And if someone doesn't like you for your stock parts, then they don't deserve a ride to begin with.

Chapter 2:

Cruising the Lots

— — — — — — — — — — — —

Some men know exactly what their "type" of woman is from the moment they pop out of the womb. Others only have the qualification that she's living and breathing. Whatever way you may want to narrow your search is your choice. After all, love may not cost a thing, but dating isn't cheap! I understand it's a small world, but you aren't in Disneyland. One ticket won't get you the whole park, and you are going to have to shell out a pretty penny on pointless dates.

When you are in the market for a new car, you tend to have your preferences. Are you looking for a specific color? Do you want an imported car, or are you looking to stay with the domestic models? You also think about more specific details: do you want an automatic or a stick, leather seats, power locks, and power windows? You have some idea of the things that are must-haves right off the bat when you are telling the salesperson what you want.

Knowing what you want comes in handy. If you want a foreign car, then you are going to check out your local foreign dealership, maybe an Audi or BMW dealer. If you want an exotic car, then by process of elimination you know you are still sticking to foreign lots, because GMC, Ford, and Chrysler can convince you why you should buy domestic, but they cannot deliver a Maybach or any other exotic car, for that matter. If you are in the market for an SUV, there's no point in test driving a Rolls Royce. Focusing on what you are looking for takes time, but it helps you when you begin your search. If you know you are into an SUV, you know you belong at a General Motors dealership where your choices will include Tahoes, Denalis, Escalades, Jimmys, and Hummers. I'll even give you Daimler with Dodge for their Durango, or Jeep Cherokee, but there's no reason for you to be in an exotic car lot if you are an SUV kind of guy. You would be wasting your time.

The same way some older guys look great driving a Corvette, others won't touch one because they think it looks better with a chick sitting it—it just doesn't fit some guys' personalities. A guy who is into blondes may not even notice when a brunette enters the room; it's just not his type. (Too bad for him!)

Know your type so you can look for it in the right places. If you are looking for a girl who is more of a homebody, why would you go to a club to try and pick one up there? If you like a girl who enjoys fine wines and exotic foods, check out your local wineries and wine-tasting events at local stores and restaurants. If you want a hot girl who likes football, check out the local bar and grills on Monday nights between September and January. You have to know *what* you are looking for so you can know *where* to look. Are you looking for a girl who can cook? A business professional? Do you care what religion she is? Figure out what's important to you in a woman. *Know your type.* If you like Asian women, tell your wingman to stop sending the blue-eyed, all-American girls your way; they're just not your type.

You may not think you really have a type. You may just love to date all kinds of women. I used to feel that way about exotic cars. I honestly thought that if I drove a car that cost more than one hundred thousand dollars, I would just love it no matter which one it was. This was until I attended a World-Class Driving event. In one weekend, I drove a Bugatti, a Lamborghini Gallardo Superleggera, a Ferrari 599 GTB Fiorano, an Aston Martin, a Maserati Quattroporte, a Spyker C8 Spyder SWB, a Mercedes SLR McLaren, a Bentley GT, and a souped-up Audi R8. Not only did I drive them, I took some up to 130 mph! I took them on windy roads to see how their traction handled. I felt out how smooth their gears shifted and how loud their engines revved. I got to admire the tiny details, such as which cars had perfect leather from cows that had been raised in separate areas so flies could never leave a flaw on their hides. I really got to know these cars inside and out.

Do you know I had the nerve to tell the owner of the Spyker I thought it was *cute* but that it really didn't do much for me? I just wasn't that impressed with it. Then I told him that when I drove the Mercedes McLaren I thought I loved it until I got in the Ferrari 599 GTB, and to be honest, I absolutely hated the half-million-dollar Mercedes McLaren. At first everyone around us thought I should be shot for saying such foul things about such a luxurious car and that I just should have felt privileged to be able to drive such fine machinery. I felt like saying, "It's just a car! Chill out, guys!"

But luckily I kept my mouth shut, and the owner of the Spyker put things into a language I could understand: dating. He turned to me and said, "Finding the right car to fit your personality is like dating. Until you find the right guy that complements your personality, you keep dating till you find him. The same way not every guy is the right guy for you, not every car fits who you are as a person." I couldn't believe we spoke the same language!

It took test-driving nine exotic cars to realize I didn't like cars that were loud and hard to handle. I had to drive nine different cars to realize I like cars with speed but need them to handle smoothly, and I don't like to feel the shifting of gears as I pick up speed. I like it to be fun, and most of all, easy to drive. When I drove the Mercedes McLaren, I was so tensed up my shoulders needed to be rubbed after I got out of the car. To press on the throttle I had to really use my core and leg muscles to get the pedal in, it was so stiff. But when I got in the Bugatti, I was relaxed, able to sit back and enjoy the car, and my knuckles weren't white from hanging on to the steering wheel tightly just to use it as leverage to give it throttle! It was just so much more delightful for me to drive. Granted, there is about a $1.4 million difference between the cars, but still, I'm just saying.

Of the nine cars I drove, my favorites were the Bugatti, the Ferrari 599 GTB, the Bentley, and the Maserati, and they all have the same dominating characteristics. They all drive smoothly and are easy to handle, and they are powerful but not obnoxiously loud. They have what I look for in a car. And they are expensive as hell!

So even if you think you don't really have a type, you probably do. Sometimes it just takes the opportunity to evaluate the dominating characteristics of the women you have dated to realize exactly what you like.

WHAT TO EXPECT FROM THE LOTS YOU ARE CRUISING

For some reason, bars are thought of as the best place to find someone. It couldn't be further from the truth, and there are tons of other places that are much better for meeting people. Now that you have figured out the type of woman you're looking for, it's time to find her. And it starts by looking in the right spots. In no particular order, there are at least seven different types of places to look, just like buying a car. There are new-car lots, certified pre-owned lots, mom-and-pop used lots, the classifieds, eBay, sold by owner, and the pick-n-pull.

At a new-car lot, you may pay a fortune, but you are also walking out of there looking sharp with the newest, fully loaded model. Certified pre-owned car lots are places where you can actually find a pretty good deal. You already know it had a previous owner, so you will receive a list of any existing problems, you can buy an extended warranty, and it isn't going to instantly depreciate five grand in value the moment you drive it off the lot—that came out of the pocket of the guy who drove it before you.

You can try the mom-and-pop used car lot, where they say "good credit or bad credit, everyone gets approved." You may pay three times the actual value of the car once you add in the sky-high interest rates. And after costly repairs, you may later find you have a salvaged title vehicle that the shady dealer had reregistered in a different state to get it cleaned. But with bad credit and no down payment, that may be the only place that will finance you.

With the classifieds, you can buy an older car from a little old lady whose cataracts have made it impossible for her to drive anymore. You'll spend three grand for a 1979 Oldsmobile with only thirty thousand miles on it. With the exception of the smell of BENGAY, you get a really great reliable car. The only downfall when it comes to classifieds is that most of the time, you don't get to see a picture, just a written description based on what the current owner's opinion is of her own car. In many cases it turns out to be a waste of time, because your opinion of a good-looking car and the current owner's opinion may be a little different. However, if you are just looking for a decent car that will get you around, you can find great commuter cars in the classifieds.

Nowadays there's eBay, where you don't even have to leave your house to find a car. This is wonderful for people who work all the time or can never find a babysitter to go jumping from lot to lot. With eBay, you just type in what you are looking for and eBay automatically gives you a list of cars that fit the description. Again, descriptions are based on the seller's opinion, but in this case, you even get to see what the seller's rating is from other customers. There are great deals to be made; just be sure you aren't bidding more than what the car is worth. This is where doing your research (for example, check out the Kelly Blue Book website, www.kbb.com, for information about a car's value) and eliminating the lemons comes in handy.

And then you have the car driving around with the "for sale" sign displayed in its window. This one is tricky—if it's driving around you know it runs, but the bad thing is that the owner is looking to get a better deal because the trade-in value must have been really bad. He is still driving this one around until he can get an upgrade. Be wary if his window is rolled down in the middle of summer—that is your first sign that some major repairs are likely needed.

If you find a car that is parked with a "for sale" sign, you may find a real beauty. You tend to find the one-of-a-kind cars when you are just driving by, not hustling from lot to lot exhausting yourself trying to finagle a deal. Maybe you're not even in the market for a new car but it just so happened that you passed by and saw something that caught your eye. Maybe you don't need a new car right now but are open to the idea should a good deal come along. You may be perfectly happy with what you have, but maybe you are in the mood to change the pace, and if you can afford it, why not? It may be fun to change things up a bit. Plus, with a parked car you can also tell that a person isn't really rushing to get rid of it because it probably means he already has another car and doesn't need the down payment for another car. This person also knows the value of the car and is willing to wait for someone to purchase it at the car's true value.

You can always have fun at the pick-n-pull. I did. I just told you that you can check out your local junkyard for a car. It may be in pieces and you may have to buy two or three cars and somehow weld them together, but yes, you can find a car at the junkyard. I have spent many hours at a whole slew of pick-n-pulls and found everything I needed when I bought two salvaged title Mustangs from the auction and put them together by buying other Mustangs from the junkyards. It was a lot of fun, and I learned a lot, but it wasn't a successful way to find a long-term car. I also rebuilt my 1990 Mustang mostly out of used parts from a junkyard, but that was just a temporary fix to needing a car.

Is any of this car talk sounding familiar? Now let's compare car lots to places where you can find women.

New Car Lots Buying a car at a new car lot is like finding a woman at Neiman Marcus. You will find a lady with class and dignity, she will be well-dressed in designer clothes, and her hands will always be manicured. She will not leave the house without looking presentable at all times. This is a woman who takes pride in making sure she is well put-together. If you find her in a designer store like Neiman Marcus, you know she is going to be high maintenance. "Mama" is going to want that new pair of shoes, with a designer name you can hardly pronounce, and Mama is probably going to want *you* to pay for them.

This woman will take great care of herself so she will always look great for you, but be prepared to shell out the big bucks and get ready to meet her best friends Louis, Gucci, and Prada. Like going to a new-car lot, if you are going to buy the newest Mercedes in stock, you're not going to drive off the lot with stock rims, are you? No way; you will probably let the salesperson talk you into buying the high-performance, run-flat tires that cost five hundred bucks a pop, and insurance, in case you get a nail in one so you can take your car in and have the tires fixed under your tire insurance policy. You certainly won't complain about only being able to take it to the dealer for oil changes. You keep it clean and drive it with pride. When it's time to make a payment you may say ouch, but you surely won't trade it in for the economy car you could have chosen to begin with. So if just reading this makes you want to complain about spending habits, meeting women at an expensive shopping mall or at a high-priced ticketed event is out of the question for you. If you like to drive expensive cars because looking good makes you feel good, and you can afford the maintenance, a high-maintenance girl is perfect for you.

Certified Pre-Owned Dealerships Say things with the girl you found to be a little too high maintenance didn't work out, and now you are in debt and without a girl. You are quick to tell your friends about the money-hungry gold digger who took you for a chinchilla coat, a Rolex, and several months of her mortgage. Your buddies are quick to bash the poor girl and one points out that his girlfriend's best friend just broke up with her boyfriend and she is great. Already knowing her, he gives you a great recommendation and reassures you that she is hot by showing you a picture. Then he and his girlfriend invite you both to their next barbeque and hope you two hit it off.

Meeting a girl through mutual friends is great way to find love. You already have something in common, so when you don't know what to talk about, you can talk about how great your friends are or reminisce about some of their funniest unforgettable moments. Plus the best part is that your wingman has already given you a full report on what type of person she is, what annoys her, and what type of guy she last dated and why they broke up—your very own dating history report.

Personally, I think this is the best way to meet a potential love interest. All of my long-term relationships have been through a mutual friend. You know exactly what you are getting into. It's like buying a car at a certified pre-owned dealership. You have someone vouching that the car you are about to buy has been through an intense inspection and has met all the requirements to be sold on that particular lot. You can ask to see a car-history report and won't find a car with more than a hundred thousand miles on it. You know it is not going to be new and may have a small ding in it here and there, but for the most part you are walking out with a great deal.

At a certified pre-owned dealership you can buy an extended warranty where the dealership will fix most problems you discover after you drive off the lot, and you'll get your car back within a couple of days.

Dating your wingman's friend is like having an extended warranty to fix your problems. If you find that you're having a problem with your girl, your friend can be a good mediator. However, like an extended warranty, there's only so much your friend can cover. If something goes wrong it's normally taken care of, but if you break it, then it's your responsibility. Your wingman will only be able to get you out of so much trouble, so don't push it. Some things are just not covered!

Mom-and-Pop Lots Let's say lady luck is not in your favor and things didn't pan out with your buddy's friend. Now you are not only broke but depressed because you feel your luck is running out. Feeling desperate, you head over to the mom-and-pop car lot where the cars actually look decent and go for a reasonable price. The salesman is really friendly and totally willing to work with your bad credit and emotional hang-ups, and he's not even going to make you show your pay stubs. Whatever you want, you got it! The BMW for two hundred and fifty dollars a month and a grand under the official Kelley Blue Book? You got it. Just sign the dotted line and the keys are yours. Wow, all before you have even opened the car door to check it out? This is too good to be true! The reason you are getting such a great deal at the mom-and-pop shop is because underneath all that Bondo holding the car together lies a serious situation.

It's a lot like meeting girls at clubs. When you first meet them, they look smoking hot, they seem sassy, fun, always up for a great time, and just carefree. Every man I know who has dated a girl he met at a club has complained about his girlfriend not being the fun gal he first met, and every woman I know has complained about her boyfriend not being the same person she first met. That is because you were both out for the night, drinking and putting on a front that you should have known you couldn't keep up forever.

It was the beer goggles that made you believe you were making out like a bandit with such a hottie, and let's not even bring up how many guys I know who shagged a girl on the first night after meeting her in a club and got her pregnant. Now you are really in a pickle. It's bad enough to find out that the super-hot babe you met at the club is really a super-hot, immature mess with a serious partying problem; it is even worse when you become legally bound to her for eighteen years!

It's like when you find out that the crooks at the mom-and-pop shop sold you a salvaged title vehicle registered from a different state and you try returning it to them. They are so great at what they do that you can't even take it back because somewhere in the fine print it said sold "as is." So you are just going to have to make the best of the situation.

TALES FROM THE ROAD

My mom once bought a car from a mom-and-pop dealership, and she was so happy with her purchase. Our car had broken down, and financially we were not able to go anywhere else to buy a car since a divorce hadn't left her with the greatest credit. The really nice, comforting salesman who owned the dealership put all her worries about being able to provide for her family aside when they got her into what he called a "semi-new" car. He didn't like to say the word "used." It was being offered at a comfortable payment plan, and she didn't have to put any money down; he accepted our old car as a trade-in for her down payment. He even towed our old car for her!

Everything was great until she brought it home. I wanted to look under the hood and pulled the lever to open it. It made a noise like it had unlatched, but it would not open. We started to wonder about our new car. We pulled a CarFax report and found out the car had been in an accident and the owner had rigged the hood to close, so now there was no way to open it. As soon as we read this, my mother drove back to the dealer. She knew that if she ever needed to put oil in the car there was no way she could have done so—the hood would not open. She tried to return the car, only to be informed that she couldn't; oh, but they *would* give her trade-in value for it if she would like to upgrade her choice of automobile.

That actually became one of the greatest moments I will never forget. Word to the wise: don't ever try to rip off a strong, stubborn Latin woman. If it wasn't for her threatening to basically bring Johnny Cochran back from the dead to represent her in court and shut down their lot, she would have had to keep the busted-up car.

*   *   *

Like the salesperson at the shady mom-and-pop dealership, meeting a woman at a club under the influence of alcohol can make you feel good about yourself and make you believe she has a lot to offer you, but once you come to find out life isn't always a party, it may be a little harder to get out of that relationship. And if you are one to have sex on the first night of meeting someone, be sure to practice safe sex; you never know when you are signing an "as is" contract that will make you legally bound to a situation for a very long time!

Meeting a girl at a club is a gamble. It is a fun place to be and it is healthy to go out every now and then, but a rule of thumb my girlfriends and I use is that we go to a club to have fun, not to meet our knight in shining armor.

Pick-n-Pulls For some inexplicable and inexcusable reason, men think they will be able to pick up chicks at happy-hour bars. Like clubs, happy-hour bars can lead you into troubled waters because they both involve one huge factor: alcohol! At least in a club you are meeting someone who is partying hard after 5:00 p.m. At a happy-hour bar, the sun has yet to go down.

In this chapter, I mention great places to meet women, but I'd like to take this time to remind you that this would be like going to a junkyard to replace a headlight cover. You might find one, but it is muggy and cracked and just not right. Sure you can get it for a bargain (in this case, let's say two beers), but it is not going to be worth all the hang-ups. Not to mention the tons of wrecked cars you have to go through to even find one in decent condition.

I have seen my fair share of junkyards, particularly when I was rebuilding my 1990 Mustang on a budget, and I will be the first to say even a great bargain from the pick-n-pull is usually only good for the first ten minutes after leaving the junkyard. If you are feeling this way about a person you met at the bar, it's because after seeing her sober—and in daylight for more than ten minutes—her true issues are revealed. This is actually the truth for men and women. There is something about dimmed bar lights that make a person's skin flawless and full of shimmer—you almost think she glistens, but later you find out it was actually just sweat. And the alcohol gives her this great outgoing and carefree personality that leads you to believe you have met the perfect person. Or if you meet her while drowning your sorrows at five in the afternoon, you think you have something in common. But outside the bar you start to think something just isn't right.

TALES FROM THE ROAD

I once managed a bar during the day that specialized in happy hour. It was so depressing that the staff secretly started calling it Lonely Hour. After working at that bar for just two months, I realized there was a common denominator in all of our regulars— everyone was lonely. I knew everyone's problems and hang-ups and for the most part everyone was brokenhearted and lonesome. During my entire time working at the bar, I can't remember one person who passed through without being there to vent about an issue. Even groups that went to a later happy hour after work were there to release tension from work.

You're not going to find a baggage-free and happy person hanging out in a bar drinking up their issues at a two dollar beer special at four in the afternoon. So if you have been using happy hour as your prime pick-up spot, it's time to broaden your horizons.

You are going to have to treat your lady like the headlight cover you found in the pick-n-pull—deal with it until you are willing to pay full price for a new one. Now don't get me wrong. Not all ladies hanging out at happy hour are damaged. If you find it appropriate to start drinking at four o'clock in the afternoon and be belligerently drunk by seven, you are probably not even complaining about your relationship. Even if your newest purchase from the junkyard has a couple of flaws, you still try to polish it and make it look its best. And when it breaks you still put money into repairing it. Better yet, you even brag about walking out like a bandit with the great deal you found. So I suggest you put just as much effort, money, and pride into your bar babe, mister! Complaining about her alcoholism or other issues is only going to complicate matters.

Hang-ups or not, she is still a lady and deserves the best. Try taking her to the late-night happy-hour bars where you get cheap food and booze from seven to eleven. Start showing her care by breaking some of her bad habits. Help her get a job where she'll work till five; then, once she has done something productive with her day, she can come home, change, and relax. Reward her with a late-night happy hour (if she's still up to it at that point). Eventually your bar babe will be over her ex, out of debt, independent, and move on to her boss, who will treat her to only fine wines. Just kidding!

The moral of the story: if you are fishing in a pool of issue-ridden swimming sharks, don't complicate a woman's life any more by complaining about her issues. Keep the hypocrisy level to a minimum because if you had your life in order, you wouldn't be drunk by seven at the same bar you met her, saving yourself three dollars per beer.

FULL COURSE YELLOW

Burnt out yet? I just gave you some pretty scary but common situations in dating. Don't give up or be discouraged; take a look at your notes and figure out what you are doing wrong. So let's take a quick break from cruising the lots.

In motorsport racing, flags are used to indicate track conditions and to communicate important messages to drivers. When a yellow flag is displayed, a driver is being warned of a caution on the track. While different racing circuits have different rules regarding their flags, it is illegal to pass another car while the course is on yellow, and all cars are required to slow down until they are given a green flag. A green flag indicates it is safe to proceed with the race. This can work to the driver's advantage, as it gives him or her a minute to regroup, and many times a driver can take the lead when the track marshal gives the green flag. Sometimes taking a minute to shake off what was a bad start is all a driver will need to get back in the game.

The greatest advice I can give anyone who is overwhelmed with not being able to find a great gal is that you date and attract people who are a resemblance of yourself. If you find yourself only dating what men love to call *crazy* women, maybe you need to take a look at why you are so attracted to every Ms. Wrong who passes you by. You attract broken women because you are, in one way or another, broken, and what you really need to focus on is fixing yourself. Men tend to escape their own issues by trying to fix someone else's. Healthy doesn't usually attract unhealthy, and when it does find someone unhealthy, you should be healthy enough to realize that if you stick around, you too will end up ailing, because misery loves company.

Buying a car can be nerve-racking, and going on ten first dates in one month can be emotionally and financially draining. But you'll get to the point where the first date will turn into a second and a third and fourth, and suddenly you have something with potential. Now let's get back to cruising the lots.

BUYING CARS ONLINE

If meeting girls at clubs and bars hasn't been working out for you, maybe you should stop partying like a rock star and take some time to stay home and get acquainted with the world of dot coms. When a woman posts her profile online, she is telling you everything about herself—that she has kids, and what her likes, dislikes, turn-ons, and turn-offs are. Everything is in front of you, just like when you are searching for a car in the classifieds. It tells you the make, model, year, mileage, whether or not it has a/c, if it runs great, needs brakes—whatever it is, all right there in front of you to read before you even make an appointment to check it out.

This is similar to how things work on an Internet dating service. She will tell you her name, body type, hair color, eye color, age, kids or no kids, what she is looking for in a man, what she enjoys for fun; it is all right there. If this one doesn't grab your attention, skip to the next one. And you didn't waste any time. Granted, sometimes the description can be a bit deceiving ... it may say "runs great," but your perception and the owner's may be two different views.

It can be the same situation when a girl says she is a well-proportioned, voluptuous, thirty-two-year-old single mother with a great career, but when you see her, the picture she had posted online was from fifteen years ago. Yikes! Better yet, she's really thirty-seven with spoiled rotten, mouthy children. And her idea of a great career is that she is a full-time mom with a part-time, afternoon notary-public gig to help her get by. Hopefully you can figure this out for yourself before you decide to go on that first date. And if not, chock it up to life experience.

If you pay to join an Internet dating site, the company that owns the website will monitor it all for you. They also guarantee their services. This is great! People are normally pleased with the service, and people who post on these sites tend to look like their pictures and normally have good jobs. I would compare this to shopping for a car on eBay. You are still getting a good deal. You may not be walking away like a bandit thinking you got a steal, but you will find a prescreened deal. And people have already rated their satisfaction with that particular seller; plus, you have a guarantee: if you don't get exactly what you read on the description of the item you were buying, you get to send it back. So sometimes it's worth the sign-up fee to join an upscale Internet dating service, knowing that what you see is what you are going to get.

DRIVING PAST A DIAMOND ON THE ROAD

Many people say that you will find the right person when you aren't even looking. When you are online, in a bar, or asking your friends to set you up, you are looking to find someone. When you are searching and searching, you can get exhausted from finding a bunch of the wrong girls. It's the same as buying a car; it is a very stressful activity. You can visit seven different car lots, look in three different magazines or newspapers, and spend a minimum of one hour searching online, and if you wake up early enough you can accomplish this in one day. By the end of the day you are so tired of talking to lying, greedy salesmen, mentally drained from not finding your perfect car in your perfect budget with the perfect mileage that it's easy to get discouraged and depressed. But remember the story in the beginning of this book about finding your dream car parked on the side of the road in perfect condition when you weren't even in the market for a car. Sure there were some problems with it down the road, but that is going to be the case in every relationship.

Sometimes, when you are least looking for a relationship, the right girl walks into your life, and since you are not putting the pressures of wanting a relationship on one another, you get to enjoy learning about each other to the fullest with no expectations. Think about it: when someone parks a car with a "for sale" sign, the owner probably has another car and isn't desperate to sell it. When the right buyer comes along, he lets go of the car at a price he is happy with. When you are just driving down the road and see a car for sale that you can't stop looking at, you'll make a call, and if the owner is great and the car sounds like something you would be interested in, you go check it out and take the deal. Just like meeting a girl when you aren't looking, you ask for her number, and if there's a spark, you ask her out.

So just keep your eyes open. Focus on yourself and what you like to do, and you never know where you might meet a prospective date. Maybe you're at a ballgame for your favorite team and you find a girl who really does love sports—and hopefully roots for the same team as you. Or maybe it's just changing your routine up a bit by trying something new. This has worked for a number of friends of mine. Maybe you've been meaning to take a jog around the park for some time now, and when you finally do, you meet a fitness buff who can show you a thing or two. And remember, no matter where you find the person you'd like to date, only pull her in with a genuine act you can keep up with. And of course there's going to be mandatory maintenance involved. But we'll get to that soon enough. Now the real work begins ...

Chapter 3:
Driver's Ed

- - - - - - - - - - - - - - -

Now that you've met someone you'd like to take out for a test drive, it's time for a pop quiz:

What do you do when you approach your car's passenger door?

You open it! Whether it's your first date or your fiftieth, open her door! When a man opens a woman's door, it's a small action that has a huge result. This chivalrous act translates to her that you thought of her first. (And if you are on that fiftieth date, thinking of her first means even more.)

At the same time, it is an act of appreciation and unselfishness for a woman to unlock or open your door from the inside. If she doesn't return the favor and this is something that is important to you, ask her to. Imply it in a simple and kind way, or even play it off as a joke if you don't feel comfortable spelling it out for her. And for the woman who did it without you even having said anything, don't forget that positive reinforcement, even a simple "thank you." Don't let our caring gestures go unnoticed.

A woman should not get into the car if a man does not open the door for her. I have stood outside the car and had a man get his lazy butt out of the driver's side to open my door. It's that important. Even if she acts coy and tells you, "Oh, you don't have to open that for me," open her door anyway; women love acts of kindness and your chivalry won't go unnoticed. It's the little things that count, especially on the first date, and even more so if you want to have a second date.

TALES FROM THE ROAD

One disastrous first date of mine that did not lead to a second should have been obvious from the "open the door" moment. Names have been changed to protect the guilty.

I met "Max" at the gym. He was in great shape, and after talking to him several times during our respective workouts, I figured we had a lot in common so I accepted his offer to go out on a date. (Remember what I said in chapter 2 about the type of lot you should be cruising. A great place to pick up a woman is somewhere you are already in your element and are naturally comfortable.)

When Max showed up at my apartment, he came to the door to pick me up, we said hello, and I was immediately excited for our date. When we got to his car, he clicked the alarm button and got in without opening the door for me. I figured he might be nervous and gave him the benefit of the doubt, and I stood outside the car waiting for him to realize he hadn't opened it. Then, instead of getting out of the car to let me in, he rolled down the passenger window and said, "Um, it's open."

I was in complete shock. "Aren't you going to open the door for me?"

His response was, "I don't open the door for anyone; it's unlocked."

At that point I had two options: I could let it go, get in the car, and make the best of it (playing it off later as a joke to show him that this was important to me), or I could thank Max for the wonderful walk to the car and head back into my home, alone. I opened the door and got in, again giving Max the benefit of the doubt, and even wondering for a minute whether I might be acting like a brat.

Biggest mistake ever! For the rest of the night, Max would only open a door if it was to let himself in first. I found myself purposely walking behind him before getting to a door so he would technically be opening the door for me. When the date finally came to an end, Max drove me back to my apartment, stopped the car in the middle of the street, started going into what a great time he had, and asked what the rest of my week was looking like for a second date. But the only words I was hearing were, "Blah, blah, blah." All I kept thinking was, *He is gearing up to give me a goodnight kiss and the car is not even in park! This tool is just going to drop me off and let me walk back to my apartment by myself!*

Max started to go in for the kiss, but he must have interpreted the look of disgust on my face in response to his drive-thru drop-off method, so he said, "I'll walk you up."

"Oh that's okay." I was testing him a bit.

You know what he said? "Okay, so I'll see you tomorrow."

I gave him a kiss on the cheek, said goodnight, slammed the door on my way out, skipped the gym the next day, and never returned one of his calls. I didn't even look back. A week or so later at the gym when he had finally figured it out and tried to apologize for not opening the door.

The moral of this disastrous first date is: you have one chance to make a first impression. Don't blow it.

Now, Pilar, you might be thinking, it's just not in my nature to open doors for ladies.

Before you even think to move forward with that thought, I'd like to share with you a great first date story where the person took the time to open the door.

I once went on a date with a guy named John. John was from out of town, so I figured that it would make sense for me to drive us around. Since he was the one to ask me out, I knew this could feel awkward, but I chose that slight moment of awkwardness over a whole night of having to give directions to someone, or even worse, sit quietly while he doesn't ask!

As we walked to the car, I went to the passenger side and opened John's door for him. He was definitely surprised and even made a comment about how weird he felt about my opening his door. This is a man who without question would open every door for me first before even thinking about himself. As I walked back around to let myself in, John reached over to open my door. It was a great start to the date, and everything from our ride to the restaurant to our dinner went off without a hitch.

After dinner, we walked back to the car, and out of habit I went to open John's door again. This time he stopped me and said, "Pilar, please stop opening the door for me. People are going to think I beat you or something; it just doesn't look right." It was obvious to me that John was so used to always showing respect for women that he saw opening the car door for a girl as an ultimate sign of respect, and he interpreted that a woman showing that much respect for a man could be taken a different way. It was cute. Awkward, but cute. I let him open my door, and he definitely got a second date.

Opening a woman's door is classy; so if it's not in your nature, pick up the habit! And I'm not just talking about the first date. Even if you've had so many dates that you've gotten to the point where she is saying, "Oh, you don't have to open it for me," it's an act of chivalry that should not be skipped.

SWEET RIDE

When your buddy gets his first sports car and brings it by so you can check out his new wheels, it is great to hear him talk about his new pride and joy. But when all he is talking about is how he can't believe how hot and sweet his new ride is, you start to roll your eyes and think, *All right already, I heard you, now can we talk about something else?*

It's the same thing for a woman. Compliments are important, but continuous, cheesy, or clichéd compliments can be quite annoying. They can make you look like you have nothing better to say, and considering how important conversation is to a relationship, that's not good at all, especially on the first date.

You see, we already know what you're going to say when you come to pick us up: "Wow, you look great!"

I don't know who came up with this line, but it must have worked well enough since every man after him thinks it's the first thing he has to say to a woman on the first date.

Once you have picked her up and opened her door, it is an appropriate time for a compliment. And if "Wow, you look great!" is the next thing to come out of your mouth, a woman is probably going to let it slide and chalk it up to nerves blocking your creativity. Try to go the extra mile by complimenting something specific about her outfit, or at least by substituting words for great. You'll notice that beautiful, wonderful, pretty, stunning—anything but great goes a long way.

She certainly went the extra mile when she was preparing for your date, so she will definitely value it when you acknowledge that you appreciate all the effort she put into looking nice to impress you. Think about those times when you spend all morning waxing your car, or when you take it to the car wash. Wouldn't you like someone to tell you how great it looks after you just spent a lot of time and effort working to make it look good? But you really only need to hear it from that one person once to get the acknowledgment you are looking for. In fact, the exact same compliment over and over in one conversation would really make you think that person is weird or obsessed with your car.

Pick the right time to compliment her, like after you've opened her door for her and gotten into the car yourself. Use that short walk around to your door as a moment to think of something original to say. And once you have said it, relax. There's no need to repeat yourself. If you're smooth about the words you choose, you'll be on a nice, smooth start to your first date.

Keep up with the compliments throughout the date; after all, who doesn't like to be appreciated? But as a rule of thumb, keep it to about three genuine compliments, five if you're Casanova. (Any more than that and she's going to wonder if something's up.)

NOTES FROM THE PASSENGER SIDE

Keep in mind that not all girls can handle a compliment, and some may even react to your acknowledging their beauty as though they're being put on the spot. I used to be that way until a man said to me, "You don't need to justify your beauty; just accept the compliment and say thank you." Those words changed my life, and I highly recommend that if you find yourself with a woman who receives your compliments with caution, feel free to use those same words.

Compliments don't only have to focus on looks. If you're planning on giving a girl three to five compliments, they'd better be good and original! Remember your buddy with the new ride. If the only thing he talks about is the six hundred horsepower, you are going to start to think that is the only thing he knows about it. Why did he buy it if the only great thing about it is the horsepower? What about the heated leather seats, the voice-activated navigational system, the cruise control, satellite radio, premium run-flat tires, keyless entry—are you catching my drift? Be observant. Tell her she is smart and funny. You can also compliment her on things such as how impressed you are by her wittiness, or her adventurous side, whatever you learn about her that makes her unique. Hopefully she has a lot more than just good looks to impress you.

One of the best compliments I have ever received was on a first date when a man turned to me and said, "Can I just tell you that I love the fact that you have your hands well manicured?" I must have had the biggest smile on my face! I spend eighty dollars a month on my manicures, and to hear that someone noticed that effort not only made me feel appreciated, but frankly, it made me think about him each time I went into the salon.

A genuine compliment is one that is not planned or rehearsed. A compliment at the beginning of the night and one during dinner will ensure that at the end of the date, she will be telling you she had a great time.

PAYING AT THE PUMP

If you don't expect your car to run on fumes alone, then you surely don't expect to have a great date with a woman without feeding her, especially on your first date. After all, when her friends call to ask her how the date went, the one thing you don't want her talking about for the next week is how she thought she had met this great guy, but then he expected her to split the dinner bill. Trust me, women will tell all their friends—and their friends' friends.

Don't get me wrong; when the bill comes at the end of dinner, drinks, or whatever, I will ask my date if he needs any money. The key here is to listen carefully to the language being used.

"Do you *need* any money?"

Not, "Here, let me pitch in," or "I'll take care of it," but "Do you need any money?" In a way, it's a test of the man's ability to provide. A woman may be prepared to pay the bill, but I can tell you that she never *expects* to pick up the tab on the first date. I'm always told to put my purse down. So when you're on a first date, and she asks if you need help with the bill, the correct answer is, "No, sweetie, I got it, but thanks for asking."

Now this does not mean that if you are hard up for cash you can't date. (Although I'd suggest being careful, because dating a woman can be as expensive as buying a car.) If you are in a financial tight spot, just be honest when you ask the girl out. Tell her that you would love to hang out with her, and you would love to take her out to dinner but hope that she'd be cool with picking up the tab for the movie. There is nothing wrong with wanting a teammate, but wait until after you have been on a few dates together.

TALES FROM THE PASSENGER SIDE

Many times I have randomly picked up the tab. After seeing a guy for a while, I'll surprise him to let him know that I appreciate all the times he's gotten the check, and it sends the message that I want to be a team player. And for any girls reading this book, let me tell you he will be so shocked and grateful that you'll feel even better about putting in your part.

I also try to get creative about how I pay the bill. I might excuse myself to the restroom and settle the tab with the waitress before heading back to the table. When he asks for the check and she says it was already taken care of, there is normally a look of immense gratitude and sweetness, which will be followed by, "Honey, you didn't have to do that." Being discreet about it helps avoid the awkward situation of putting a man in the position to try and talk you out of paying because he feels obligated to take care of you. It's important in a relationship for each party to take turns taking care of each other. And always say thank you!

*   *   *

Now guys, the trick here is to never expect women to pick up the tab, and when they do, don't make a big deal about it, but definitely show them how wonderful it was of them. Girls love to help out when they are not expected to. But remember: only friends go Dutch. If you're in a financial jam, consider taking turns treating each other on every other date. But if over-the-top expensive dates are putting you into a financial hardship, it's time to consider the same question you did when you were considering a Lexus versus a Honda: Is high maintenance really my thing? Some girls will not be okay with paying at all. If your car is used to premium gas and you suddenly start to give it regular, it may not run so well for you. So if the woman you're dating has no intention of pitching in, it's time to consider whether you want to pick up a second job to foot the bill or let her go if you can't keep up with her needs. (If you're finding yourself in this situation more than a few times, it's time to revisit chapter 1.)

PERFORMANCE ANXIETY

Imagine you have just driven off the lot with the first sports car you have ever owned. The anxiety is building to push your new car to the max. The first chance you get, you hit the road with no intentions other than taking it to the limit. You're anxious to take the top down and feel the gravitational force pull your cheeks back to your ears, to feel the rush of your right foot slamming the pedal to the medal, the vibration of your V8 giving you everything it's got. And it feels great!

Suddenly, a bunch of tumbleweed is looking you right in the eye. You swerve to avoid it but end up losing control, and just your luck, a pothole causes you to flip your brand new car. You were so anxious that you couldn't wait to find a safer road so you let your hormones and testosterone lead you, and you turned a test drive into a disaster!

This scenario may sound a bit extreme, but that is exactly how crucial a first kiss can be. Just like with compliments, it is all about timing. Depending on the circumstances that led to the date, the type of girl you are taking out, and what you have planned for the date, the appropriate time to plant one on her differs with each situation. While some women like to wait toward the end of the date for a kiss, some won't kiss at all on the first date, and others like kissing at the beginning of the date to alleviate some of the pressure. Use your judgment.

Should you find the situation appropriate to kiss her at the beginning of the date, make it tasteful. Think sweet and cute. Remember, this is awfully brave of you—she could be easily offended and think you have the wrong impression of her. Take the right steps to make your first kiss a success.

Hopefully, you're going to her place to pick her up. Walk to the door with flowers. You don't need a whole arrangement or a table centerpiece; something with a couple of red or pink roses and a nice variety of other flowers is perfect. When picking flowers, always remember: a dozen roses are a cliché and half a dozen roses are a cheap cliché. Please note that the supermarket manager's special of assorted flowers is just as cheap. The keyword to always keep in mind is "chivalry." When she answers the door, greet her with flowers. In your own words say hello, and don't forget to smile. As you hand her the flowers give her a small peck on the cheek just to play it safe. Almost as if you have been friends for years. If she's okay with the kiss, she will let you know by kissing you back. It's a process; remember, you still have all night. So don't let your hormones get ahead of you.

For those of you who plan on waiting until the end of the date to kiss, don't sweat the entire date waiting for the perfect moment. Be cool and calm, and don't stress about it. If you find the appropriate moment, you find it; if you don't, then just hope for a second date. You may have been expecting me to tell you to wait for a goodnight kiss. That's about as predictable as, "Wow, you look great," and for the most part it's so rehearsed it feels mechanical. You walk her to her door; tell her what a wonderful time you had; she agrees. You express wanting to see her again, she agrees, and you say goodnight, she responds goodnight. You both smile and feel so awkward that the expressions show on your faces, essentially ruining that moment you have spent all night building up to. You have waited so long (and are now ready to explode) that all you end up having is a really tense moment, or worse, a really awkward kiss.

If you're waiting until the end of the date to kiss her, just make sure not to wait until the very last moment. Take a chance and hope for the best. If you do it right, you'll have a bit of time before the end of the date to kiss some more and see whether there's chemistry, and at the end of the night you will automatically get a goodnight kiss.

That being said, if you notice she isn't into you, don't force the issue. I had a guy try to kiss me one time and I was so not into him that when he went to kiss me, I involuntarily shut my lips as tight as I could. If you haven't been giving each other the "I-want-to-kiss-you" eyes yet—you know what I mean—and you aren't sure, be cordial about it and ask her if she minds you giving her a kiss. I always think that is cute and extremely respectful. Always start with just a peck and let it evolve naturally.

Remember, if you don't familiarize yourself with the road first, you won't know how it turns, and you will only leave yourself open to losing complete control of the situation.

CALLING THE MECHANIC

It's time to debunk the myth of the phone call. You know which one I'm talking about. Wait three days once she gives you her number to call and say hello, wait half a day to call her back, wait till the next day after the first date to call her again. Only call once if she doesn't pick up the first time you call.

I'll bet that when you leave your car at the mechanic and he tells you that you can call after 3:00 to come pick it up by 5:00, you don't wait until 4:30 to call and make sure the car will be ready. Of course not! By 3:15 max, you are on the phone calling to make sure your precious car will be ready. You don't wait for the mechanic to call you; you're already on the phone long before your car is even supposed to be ready. It's time to apply the same theory to dating. If you had a great date, call her on your way home.

Here's an idea of how this conversation might go:

You: Hey, I just wanted to let you know that I had a great time tonight.

Her: Me too. I had a lot of fun.

You: Well, I just wanted to say goodnight, and sweet dreams.

Her: Thanks, have a safe ride home.

You: Thanks, I'll give you a call sometime tomorrow. Goodnight.

You get off the phone knowing what your next step is, and she gets off the phone and calls her best friend to brag about what a great time she had—and how you didn't wait to call, how she doesn't have to wonder when you'll call next, and she will already be looking forward to your call the next day.

It's all about taking initiative. Girls want you to call them. We want to feel desired. Frankly, we want to be chased even after we've been caught. This leads me to our next topic: the morning-after phone call.

Whether you waited for a period of time or hooked up on the first date, whether you just messed around or had crazy wild sex till six in the morning, make sure she gets the morning-after call. There is a sense of reassurance that comes with this phone call. A sense of not feeling used for the night and never called again. Even if you never see the girl again, it still puts her at ease, eliminating the *Man, I can't believe I put out, I'm such a sucker, that's all he really wanted!* thoughts. Believe it or not, most girls care about what a guy thinks, and most girls want you to respect them.

Please let me make it clear that the morning-after phone call is not to boost her ego. I have had many guy friends ask me why they should call a girl they never plan to see again just to satisfy her ego. It has nothing to do with her ego; it is her self-esteem that gets hurt. Even if you never plan to see her again or you feel that if a woman wants to be respected, she should respect herself, does it really take that much out of you to be kind for one minute to make sure her self-esteem is not hurt? No, it does not.

Think about when you take your car into the dealership for service. Taking your car to the dealership versus Don's Auto Repair for an oil change is going to cost you double. But you know that phone call you get from your friendly dealership a couple of days later to make sure you were happy with your service and your car is running perfectly? It eliminates that feeling of being suckered. The guys at Don's may have been cheaper, but the guys at the dealership care. The morning-after phone call gives a woman the same feeling. It's important that you care—even if you're not interested in pursuing a relationship, and all the more important if you are. Look guys, it is not cool to be mean or disrespectful to a woman by making her feel bad. Especially after sex, since what she was really trying to do was please you. So make the morning-after call a new habit if it is not already on your agenda.

ON APPROVED CREDIT

Nothing sucks more than wanting to buy a car so badly and then knowing you are going to have to "qualify" to take it home or "qualify" for all the great rebates and APR. The reality is that many times, a salesperson will come back to the table after running your application and give you the words you hoped you wouldn't hear: "I'm sorry, sir, but your application was denied; the banks thought your credit rating was too low."

Regardless of how gently the salesperson breaks the bad news to you, it still sucks. Especially after you spent all afternoon test driving and bonding with the car. The truth is that no matter how upset the news makes you, you handle yourself with class and dignity. You don't get crazy and mad and start throwing things or kicking the cars, and I certainly hope you would not start begging the salesperson to talk to his supervisor and check your great work history because you can really afford the car with no problem. There is a certain way to handle rejection, and if you let your ego and emotions take control, you are probably going to make the salesperson or someone else at the car lot call the police.

Handling yourself with class and dignity is the same way you should handle yourself when a girl tells you she has really enjoyed talking to you all night at the bar, but you really aren't her type or she is seeing someone but is flattered by your offer. Or even more painful is when you have been spending time with a girl and after taking her out on several dates that have cost you a handful of hard-earned dollar bills, she tells you she really enjoyed spending time with you but doesn't see things going any further.

This actually reminds me of a time that one of my friends bought a brand new Mustang. After driving it around for two full weeks, the dealership called him and told him the bank declined his application and that he had to return the car immediately but would be refunded his down payment. At least in this case the dealership returned his investment, but the fact that he was going to have to explain to his friends why he didn't have his new ride anymore was going to be a painful blow to his ego. To his credit, he gracefully returned the car. He thought about racking up the miles on it just out of spite, but he put his ego in check, returned the car, and told the salesperson, "Thanks for letting me have a free car to drive for the last two weeks."

I see people lose their cool constantly when a girl rejects them. Of course, no one likes to be rejected, but you cannot force someone to go home with you or think you're sexy or want to date you. If she doesn't want to be with you, you need to handle rejection with class. Don't take it personally. For whatever reason, she thought your application wasn't in her best interest at that time. She gave it a shot and was honest enough to tell you things were not working out. So be cool with her decision. Don't let your ego get you into trouble.

I was at a bar once with a friend, and standing next to us was a very pretty group of girls. It was only a matter of time before a group of guys built up the courage to talk to them. One of the guys was buying one of the girls drinks all night. When the rest of her friends were ready to leave, she went to say goodbye to the guy, and he asked her to stay. He told her that she could stay the night in his hotel and that he'd make sure she got home in the morning. She very politely smiled and declined his offer. He proceeded to persist and borderline beg. She still declined.

Finally he snapped. This man became aggressive and started yelling, calling her a tease and other vulgar names in front of his buddies at the bar because his ego was hurt that she would not go home with him. It became so bad that security escorted the guy out of the bar, which only made him angrier because he was the one who had been spending money there, not her.

I can see where he got frustrated, and maybe she shouldn't have taken drinks from him all night, but that does not give anyone the right to act out of line because she didn't want to go home with him.

And please don't handle rejection by sleeping with one of our friends. That is just your ego trying to get revenge. Always keep your ego in check, because we are on to you with this one. We know you only slept with our friend because your feelings got hurt and you were looking to one-up us, not because you found her attractive.

TALES FROM THE ROAD

A close friend of mine actually tried dating me when I first met him, but I was not thrilled about his profession due to the amount of travel involved. In this case his "bad credit" was that I didn't like his job. I explained that I just wasn't at a point in my life where I wanted to date someone who traveled as much as he did. He and I were at an event, and he saw me exit the venue with a guy who just happened to be a friend of mine. He was talking to another girl and got so angry seeing me leave with another guy that he didn't even acknowledge me. Later that night, while my friend and I met the rest of our group at another venue, he decided to sleep with one of my girlfriends. This man was so "over me" and was really going to show me by hooking up with one of my friends, not even caring whether or not I found out.

The next night I ran into my guy friend again, and once again we were having a great time. Just when he had me convinced he wasn't like the rest of the guys in his profession, my girlfriend came storming up to him demanding he explain himself for sleeping with her and not returning her calls the next morning.

I can see where he thought if I wasn't interested in him, he would find another girl, just as he would buy a $14,000 car if he couldn't get approved for a $20,000 car. The logic makes sense, but not if the only reason you are buying the $14,000 vehicle is to show the salesman you can get a car. So it would have been no problem had this man hooked up with any other girl, but it became a problem when he hooked up with my friend, because girls stick together. Of course I was going to take her side and think he was a dog for sleeping with her and not calling her. Had he really liked her, I would have been happy for them, but he wouldn't even return her calls the next morning. Sleeping with our friends is not the best way to handle rejection.

I'll give you a better scenario with a happy ending. One year I was working at a Playboy golf event, and while I was helping the staff check in golfers, there was one golfer who was obnoxiously loud and crotchety. His golf clubs had gotten lost, and on the way to the golf course the driver got lost. This man had been sitting in LA morning traffic, and his nerves were shot. He cut in front of every golfer to demand that someone find his clubs. I asked him to calm down, but there was no calming this man. We got him situated, and off to the course he went. Every time I saw him on the course that day he was whining and yelling about one thing or another. I thought this man actually had anger issues. The golf scramble ended with a huge party at the Playboy mansion, and everyone had a little too much to drink and tried to hook up before the weekend was over.

I saw this guy several times at the party, and he asked me out, but due to the behavior I saw earlier, I responded with, "I don't date guys I meet here." Luckily his ego and anger didn't take over in *that* situation, because I guarantee I would have never forgotten what it would have looked like if a Playboy security guard would have dragged him out. He kept his cool and went about the party, and I am sure found a backup girl to take home. (There's someone for everyone.) A year later I saw him again at the same event, although he was having a much better day than the first time I met him, and we even laughed about his behavior the year prior. As I got to know him I actually thought this guy was charming. But what really made him stand out was when he mentioned he still hadn't forgotten how I had turned him down a year ago. I didn't remember him asking me out, and when he reminded me of my response about not dating people I meet at these events, I put my foot in my mouth by saying, "I did? That's a lie! I date people I meet here all the time." I saw the expression on his face kind of change, and I thought things were going to get ugly, but he kept his cool. As the night progressed I ended up really liking him and was so impressed that he didn't hold a grudge against me for rejecting him a year ago that he ended up with my number before the weekend was over. We dated for a while and are now great friends.

*   *   *

There is always a risk that a girl is not going to want to have a second date or continue to see you. However, just like handling yourself at the car lot bargaining table when the salesperson tells you the bank does not want to do business with you, handle yourself with class, because there are two ways it could end: by being asked to leave or escorted out by security, or by getting a car once you clear up your credit.

DEFENSIVE DRIVING

From opening the door to the goodnight phone call, treat every date as if it was your first and just watch what a wonderful time you will have on all your date nights.

Chapter 4:
Regular Maintenance

— — — — — — — — — — — — —

Let's say you finally found something worth leasing. You'd like to take the time to drive it a while to see if you will love it so much that one day you'll just decide to go all out and buy it. (Or maybe after a while you'll decide that maybe it isn't the right car, just the right car for the moment.) Regardless, spending more time than just a test drive with any car will result in one thing: car trouble. It's what they do best.

Let's say you find a girl you really like and things go so well with her on the first date that you take her out again. One thing leads to another, and suddenly you two love birds are starting to see each other on a regular basis. This is fantastic. You're feeling like a teenager all over again, and it's probably due to all those long make-out sessions, all the time you're spending together, and the fact that your friends think you two are the greatest couple ever. Plus, she doesn't nag, and you don't fight over not returning her phone calls in a timely manner.

It's like when you first drive your new car off the lot. You are glowing with joy. You want to show all your buddies your new ride, you become the designated driver just because you want to drive your car all the time, you get all giddy when you tell your parents you finally found your perfect car, and best of all, you aren't going to have to deal with any maintenance issues for at least three thousand miles. It's great at first, but there will come a time or two that the car payments might double up, or you might hit a curb too hard and pop a tire. Accidents will happen, and you will have to roll with the punches. You won't be able to take the car back just because a new model came out or the tires pop too easily or the payments are too high at the moment. If you got sick of a problem and traded in your car every time, you would quickly realize what I mentioned earlier—all cars are going to give you some kind of trouble. Regardless of whether it's a German, American, Swiss, French, or Japanese model—no matter who made your car, it's time to learn to make the best of bad times.

It's just like dating the same woman for a while. There are plenty of benefits to steadily dating someone. You get to grow with her, laugh at inside jokes with her, she will start to take care of you the way you do for someone you care about, and sex gets better as you become more and more comfortable with each other. But after a while it's also common to enter a comfort zone—and that's when the nagging begins. You may get annoyed with the sudden loss of bliss, but you are just going to have to write it into the budget. If you dump a girl every time you hit a bump in the road, you are going to end up one lonely man, and I assure you that whether it is over a big or small issue, every relationship is going to have them, and often more than one. On the plus side of things, like a car, there are some things you can do to avoid a lot of problems.

To avoid the nagging, here are some prime relationship maintenance tips:

DUI: DIALING UNDER THE INFLUENCE

Friends don't let friends drink and dial! There is nothing more annoying to a girl than being woken from peaceful beauty sleep to hear her man drunk with a bunch of guys in the background, slurring words she can't even understand. The worst is when a man starts to talk dirty to a girl while he is drunk and leaving a club and probably had some other girl grinding up all over him throughout the night.

Guys, when you are drunk, you lose the filter that keeps you from saying things that are probably better kept as your own private thoughts. Sometimes this can result in sharing with the guys those intimate bedroom moments that were meant for keeping between you and your girl. Brutal honesty is also a great way to get yourself into trouble if you were misbehaving at any point throughout the night. If your girl asks you about something you'd prefer to keep from her, you aren't going to be able to tell a believable lie. Your designated driver for the evening should also be on cell phone duty. Text messaging, Tweeting, and use of all other social media networks including Facebook are also considered "dialing," so avoid that as well. Even if you think you are being sweet and cute, unless you are 100 percent aware of who and what you are text messaging, save it for the morning.

IF YOU DON'T RUSH THE CARWASH
GUY, DON'T RUSH ME EITHER

I dare you to rush the person washing your car at the carwash. See what you end up with. You will have streaks all over the place. You will still see the brake dust on your wheels, and the crumbs in your cup holder will still be there.

The mood you will put your woman in by rushing her is not worth ruining your night just because she took an extra half hour to look extra great. Don't call her if she isn't at your house yet, and if she is getting ready at your house, don't barge into the bathroom when she is trying to finish getting ready. You are invading her space and are going to get yelled at. Women require time to get ready, and there is nothing you can do about it.

Sure we have an estimated time that it will normally take us to get ready, but that time slot does not allow any room for a change of mind or a change of wardrobe. An hour is a fair time allowance for a woman to get ready; however, when we are under pressure and feel the need to look extra special for the occasion and for our man, it is absolutely normal for a girl to take some extra time should she change her mind about her wardrobe. Not to mention extra *extra* time for those times we feel fat in our outfit! That will definitely throw a monkey wrench in our whole night.

A girl needs to feel pretty to act pretty. When a woman is feeling like she is not thin, or she is out in public and doesn't really love her outfit, her attitude will show it. When a woman feels beautiful and sexy, she will behave that way. I hate to go out when I can't find anything in my closet that doesn't fit me perfectly. In fact, when I am feeling fat, I wear sweats and don't even waste the energy trying to find something to wear. And when I feel fat and dress in sweats, the *last* thing I want to do is come home after dinner and make love. But if I am allowed enough time to get ready and I feel I look great, then I feel sexy, and at that point I can't wait to come back home to give my man some lovin'.

Rushing a woman will get you nowhere. A woman knows what time she is supposed to be ready and knows that if that time slot is crucial, she does not mean to run late; in fact, she is twice as frustrated as you are over the lateness. So grab a drink and relax so she can peacefully get ready. After all, if she didn't care about impressing you, she would have been ready the moment she rolled out of bed. And when she is finally ready, you know how much *time* and effort she has put into looking nice, so when she is finally ready be sure you tell her how beautiful she looks. And when she apologizes for her tardiness, let her know it was worth the wait.

KEEP THE HIGH-PERFORMANCE GAS IN THE TANK; A.K.A. NEVER STOP DATING

Getting to know someone is exciting. Going on fun dates is exciting. Thinking about them throughout your day is exciting. Unfortunately, as time goes on, those things become routine, or worse, they lessen, and the feeling of excitement turns into boredom. This is normal and will happen with anyone you date for more than three months. You're bound to hit a comfort zone. This is the point when you begin to feel as though your relationship is in a state of stagnant blah. Don't worry, this isn't a bad sign for your relationship but an opportunity. You have the power to put some excitement back into your life.

When you first buy a new car, you put premium gasoline in the tank. And you swear you will never use regular unleaded in your new car because you want to give it only the best for the best performance. You would rather walk than pump 87 percent octane into your gas tank. You love how easily your car can pick up speed with the higher octane gasoline. So you continue to buy the premium gas, cruising around and loving your new car. As summer approaches, and we all know gas prices increase, you may downgrade to super-unleaded fuel. After all, premium has 92 percent octane and super has 90 percent octane, so what will a 2 percent difference matter? Now as you are driving, you notice that your car doesn't go up a steep hill as smoothly as it used to, but no big deal: you are still getting up the hill without causing a traffic jam.

Sooner or later it's the middle of the summer and gas prices are starting at four dollars and fifteen cents a gallon. You figure all the car really requires is unleaded fuel anyway, it isn't like the car requires premium unleaded (some cars, like Audis, will only take premium gas so you will never have a chance to slack). So you do what you swore you would never do and pump 87 percent octane into your precious car. You come to the bottom of that steep hill and realize you need to turn off the air conditioner because otherwise you are really struggling to get to the top. Had you pumped your gas tank with regular unleaded gasoline from the start, you never would have thought it would be an issue to get up the steep hill. This doesn't mean you should have used regular from the start, it just means you wouldn't have known it could have been better. But now you know you have had better since you started off giving your car only the best. It used to be fast and fun, and getting up a steep hill was something you never put much thought into. You got used to your car having a certain rhythm, and when you gave it gasoline with lower octane, it gave you less performance, less excitement.

This is exactly what happens when your relationship turns stagnant and bland. You used to take your lady dancing. You would have her get dressed up for a nice dinner or a fun night on the town. You two can tell funny stories for days about the fun you used to have in the beginning. What happened to all that excitement? You got comfortable. You stopped dating when she became your girlfriend. Had you begun to give your car the premium gasoline again, the performance would pick up, and before you knew it, driving up the hill with your air conditioner on would be fine. This is the same approach you should take with your relationship. Now! Do it the minute you notice things are starting to lurch along. Let me tell you, you're likely to notice *after* she has noticed there is a problem, so you need to take action immediately. Ask her on a date and keep all the tips in mind from chapter 3 to charm her again by bringing back the exhilaration of dating. Dating will get her excited about the relationship again, and by experiencing her genuine enthusiasm, it will rub off on you.

TALES FROM THE ROAD

Trust me on this one. I dated a guy for six-and- a-half years and we eventually broke up because there was nothing really keeping us together. We loved each other, but spending time with one another became boring. There were chores I would rather have done than spend an evening at home with him. When we broke up we missed each other and tried dating again, but he was still too comfortable. He never offered to take me out. I would remember how, when we first started dating, he would take me on spontaneous day trips to the beach or a bed and breakfast. I would remember going to clubs and getting so drunk we would have a taxi take us home. Even our time at home was fun at first. We would cook and have some wine while we played a board game by the electric fireplace.

But even when we missed each other so much and said we would do anything to try and save our relationship, we just couldn't bring the fun back into it. We had been using regular unleaded for too long. Finally we had a conversation about our boredom, and he realized what was missing. He realized that in the beginning he would do so many things with me. We would go biking, hiking, running, and shopping, or we'd surprise each other at work for a random lunch. It wasn't only the trips, it was all the things we would do to let the other person know we were thinking of each other that kept us giddy. He'd send me flowers just because; I'd send him a card in the mail when even I knew I was going to see him every day. I had been pointing him toward this realization for months, but one day he had this great epiphany of trying to date me again. I shut my mouth and let him believe he came up with that one all on his own, and suddenly we started laughing all the time. We stopped fighting, and that feeling of excitement came back.

*   *   *

Dating is what gives performance to the relationship. It keeps things fun and different. It is identical to octane—you give 92 percent octane in the beginning and you will have exceptional performance. It's when you cut corners and get comfortable and only pump 87 percent octane into it that you start struggling. Give your relationship your all and trust me, you will see it in the performance.

YOU DON'T LET PEOPLE DING YOUR CAR, SO DON'T LET THEM DISRESPECT YOUR WOMAN

I was sitting around the kitchen once with a man I was dating and some of his buddies. We were having a great time cooking dinner together and trying to top each others' funny stories. One of his friends had been a boxer for quite some time and was now a trainer, so he was a fairly huge man, very intimidating. He was telling us a story he found funnier than I did: when he was living in Australia there was a problem on his street with kids vandalizing other people's cars. One night he heard the kids outside and saw that they were close to his car. He proceeded to tell us how he beat up the kids before they even touched his car—to teach them a lesson.

I was taken aback since it was clear they hadn't even touched his car, and I said so. He went on to say that the lesson learned was very valuable—don't mess with a man's car. He obviously felt that by taking action before the kids even touched his car, they would think twice about vandalizing someone's property. I continued to argue my point, because to me, the violence was unjustified and sounded more like bullying.

And then I was caught completely off-guard by the quote of the century. The man I was dating jumped in to defend his friend's actions, and said, "What are you talking about, Pilar? He didn't overreact by kicking their asses. I would have done the same thing. Some punk vandalizing your car is worse than some punk raping your girlfriend!"

Now, if you couldn't tell from the title and subject matter of this book, I have no problem comparing cars and women. But in this case, I almost choked in shock that he would even compare the two. A car is a materialistic item that can be replaced. If it is vandalized, your insurance policy will pay for the repairs, end of story. If a woman is raped, you can't cash in on your insurance policy to get her fixed and erase the damage. Plus, this man standing up for his friend and the rights of his car was the same guy who wouldn't do a thing when guys would shout "Hey baby!" at me when we were out in public. And I don't mean he ignored them the way you are supposed to. I mean he didn't even notice them.

Failing to make sure your woman is respected is the quickest way to cause a blowout in your relationship. So you can imagine what his quote of the century did in that case.

You should be making your woman your priority. Now when I say making her your priority, I do mean in every aspect of your life. She will want to be your number-one pick when it comes to spending time with her, coming to her defense, listening to her when she needs to vent, taking care of her when she is sick and, most importantly, respecting her—even in front of the guys.

I'm not saying to be a pushover, but trying to look like you wear the pants just to impress the guys is only going to earn you a trip to the dog house. If someone is making her feel uncomfortable—even if it's your buddy—you should stick up for her like she was as defenseless as your parked car out in a cold, dark alley. This doesn't just apply to disagreements at dinner either. If your guys want to go out but you already made plans with your girl, guess what? You're keeping your plans with your girl. That is unless the guys have VIP tickets to a car show or some other once-in-a-lifetime opportunity. If you do decide to change your plans to be with your boys, you can be sure you will get the speech that starts off with, "I am the least of your priorities. I changed my night around to spend time with you and now you want to hang out with the guys? What am I? Where do I stand?"

If you value your woman like the guy from the story values his car, you will make sure to always take your girlfriend's feelings into consideration—especially around other people. Make her feel like she is at the top of your priority list, even when she may know she is not. Rihanna said it best in her hit single "Only Girl" where she said, "I want you to love me like I'm a hot ride." Although I do find that statement very appropriate, in the first line to the chorus, Rihanna belts, "Want you to make me feel like I'm the only girl in the world." The truth is, guys, your woman is well aware that your career and family (and sometimes even freedom) truly come first, but if you always make her feel like you have her back, she will know that you respect her and will in turn treat you with the same respect. This really boils down to less nagging about not making her a priority in your life.

MODERN CARS THAT CAN DO IT ALL THEMSELVES

While we are talking about respect, I find this is the perfect time to bring up chick empowerment. I talk a lot about respecting a woman and always putting a woman ahead. As old-fashioned as I am, times have changed, and women have become more independent. Some guys love this movement and some guys hate it. Even the guys who love it find a self-sufficient woman wonderful until he feels she doesn't need him. Do you want me to let you in on a little secret? Women may not *need* a man, but it sure is nice to have a man in our lives. The key to making this work is balance. You want a woman to be independent, and you should encourage her to be self-sufficient and to always have an opinion. Whether it is right or wrong doesn't matter as long as it is her own opinion and her own voice. You want her to be a teammate, not a team-mooch. You should want and encourage a well-rounded woman; it makes her easy to approach in every situation. You won't have to babysit a self-sufficient woman in a room full of people, as she will be able to mingle with strangers and not feel intimidated with new surroundings.

You want a woman who is like a Range Rover. The Range Rover is your perfect every-situation car. You can take the kids to soccer practice in it; you can run around town in it; you can pile all your friends into it and go camping or load up some snowboards and hit the snow. You can also off-road in it, and at the end of all your adventures, you can drive it through a carwash and it is the perfect car to take to a nice dinner date or work meeting. Heck, you can even show up to a red-carpet event in a Range Rover!

This is what you should encourage your woman to be—the every-situation girl. She doesn't have to be a know-it-all to know a little about everything. Encourage her to grow so that she can blend into any situation. If she's strong enough to hold her own, she will be the perfect date for any occasion, just like a Range Rover.

On the flipside, many times this backfires on a guy, and a man ends up feeling emasculated by a woman's independence. It ends relationships all the time. It is important to let your woman know that no matter how strong she may be she can always count on you, because as her man, you will always be just a little bit stronger.

This isn't a power struggle, this is a trust struggle.

When a woman feels she needs to provide for herself and her family, she becomes very strong very fast. Her focus is on being a provider and always being able to handle anything, and she loses focus on being a woman. A successful woman always has to prove herself at work because she is always fighting for one thing or another. This will cause her to become callused, and she may start to lose her softness. Sometimes she may even bring work home with her and may be defensive with you because that is how she has to be at work all day. This is when it is easy for a woman to unintentionally make her man feel like everything but a man.

The solution to this is in your hands. Let your woman know that no matter how strong she may have to be at work, when she is with you, you are strong enough for her. This way, when she gets home, instead of thinking about all the responsibilities that need to be taken care of, she can focus on being a woman—*your woman.* Let her know it is okay to be a "damsel in distress" because you won't leave her stranded. Think of it like the paddle-shifting technology in the Jaguar XKR. I use the Jaguar as an example because this is one I am very familiar with, but these days pretty much all cars have paddle shifters. The paddle-shifting technology in the Jaguar is amazing! I am able to drive the Jaguar as a manual using paddle shifters, but with all the technology Jaguar has put into its engineering, when the rpms get too low in the judgment of the computer, I can trust the Jaguar's transmission to automatically downshift for me even if I am in manual mode. So if I have to suddenly brake but forget to downshift, the technology in my Jaguar has got my back.

This is exactly what a woman wants from her man. We want to be able to trust that our man can step up when something is too heavy for us to lift on our own. Women want a man who can be strong enough for us when life makes us too weak to be able to stand on our own. If you cannot show your woman that you are strong enough to be her man, she will find the "man" within herself and become a wo-*man*. This is where you will feel she doesn't need you, because you have left her no choice but to always fend for herself.

TALES FROM THE ROAD

The best example that comes to mind was when I dated a man who was very well aware of my independence and even loved that I would remodel my own house. He also loved that I tore down and rebuilt an entire wall in my condo. He was at my house one day, and I had just bought a new picture frame that I was anxious to hang. When he saw me walk into the living room with a hammer, he smiled and asked, "What are you doing?"

I replied, "Hanging my picture."

He said, "Awww! That's really cute, but I'll do it."

Without hesitation I replied, "It's okay, I can do it."

His response was, "I know you can, baby, but I will hang your picture for you."

Can I tell you how sexy I found it when this man walked up to me, gently took the hammer from my hands, and hung my picture for me? He let me know at that moment he loved that I was a strong and independent woman, but as long as he was around, he was always going to be the man in our relationship.

MANDATORY MAINTENANCE

There are certain things in life that are unavoidable. Changing your oil every three thousand miles, pumping gas when your tank hits empty, changing your brake pads before you wear them down to the rotor, rotating your tires—you get the idea. Sometimes you may dread taking care of these mandatory maintenance requirements because you are short on cash or time. Like when you are already late and know you don't have enough gas in your tank to get to your destination, but you're still contemplating not stopping at a gas station. Deep inside you know that if you do not take the ten minutes to pump some gas into your car, it's going to stall. Or if you don't change your oil, it's going to run out and then you're going to blow your engine. Sometimes, with necessary items that are quite costly, like changing brakes, you try to put off the grinding noises until the timing is a little more convenient for the wallet. But when you get around to taking care of business, you realize that by now you've worn down the rotors from the lack of cushion the new brake pads would have provided. What would have cost you two hundred dollars is now a whopping half a grand!

Do you get my point, or do I need to talk about the blowout you can cause from not putting air in your tires? These mandatory maintenance requirements are normally written down for you in the instruction manual that comes with your car. There is normally a guide that will have it all charted out for you: what to do when your car hits five thousand miles, ten thousand miles, and twenty thousand miles. When you go to get your oil changed every three thousand miles (older cars), five thousand miles (some new cars), or ten thousand miles (in some Jaguars), whoever serviced your car always puts a little sticker on your windshield that tells you when your next oil change should be. And for the most part, even if you hate it you still get it done. Why? Because you have to and you even have it written down for you in your manual, so you know that if you don't pay attention to these regularly scheduled maintenance issues, you're simply going to ruin your car.

It's important to follow the guidelines in your manual, and the almighty manual to relationships with the opposite sex isn't mythical. It's a calendar! You don't even have to run out and buy one because you already have one if you have a cell phone, BlackBerry, iPod, computer, etc.—so you're probably carrying around at least one at all times. Now put it to work for you!

Most calendars are already marked with all the important dates for you. The only two that are missing are her birthday and your anniversary, so fill in the blanks. Now that you have *all* the important dates in your calendar—and maybe even a reminder about each one a week beforehand—repeat after me: important dates are meant to be celebrated. If it is on the calendar and Hallmark has a card for it, celebrate it.

If you live by this rule of thumb, you will never forget an occasion. Now that you are covered in remembering every occasion, don't shoot yourself in the foot by not making it special. Women like to feel that you put time and effort into picking a gift. (This is where the reminder a week beforehand comes in handy.) No matter how long you have been together, you never get over the card-and-flower phase of the relationship. Remember to handwrite a sweet note on the card. Show her that you care. I would rather have a small bouquet of flowers and a sweet card with a man's endearing words than an overwhelming arrangement of flowers and a card that just said Happy Birthday with his name printed by the florist. It really isn't the size of the gift; it's the size of the thought behind the gift.

Now flowers and a card are still part of the remembering phase that normally won't be considered a gift in most cases. It's better than nothing, but flowers and a card are you just telling us, "Hey, look, I remembered! Happy anniversary!" Sorry guys, I know you probably feel like we are just so hard to please, and I understand, but I am just being honest with you—flowers and a card won't be enough. I didn't make us this way. Chock it up to our emotional genetic makeup or the chick flicks we have been watching since we were teens. We have come to want you to go the extra mile to really make us feel special. And you know what they say, "If you can't beat them, join them." You have to. It's like when you take your car for an oil change and the guys at the shop tell you that you need a list of fluids in your car to be filled as well. Just because you remember to give it new oil doesn't mean that's all it needs. So spend a little more time and a little more money and get her gifts that can be unwrapped.

NOTE FROM THE DRIVER'S SEAT

I once dated a guy who told me that for my birthday present, he was going to take me shopping. It was a nice idea, but the problem was he told me the night before my birthday, which made me feel like he had forgotten it. He made a valid point stating that had he gone shopping without me I would have only gotten one or two outfits, but instead he would not only be taking the time to go with me to try on the outfits, I would get at least four outfits because he would have thought everything looked great on me.

Flattery goes a long way, and he felt that he had made a good case against my feeling like he hadn't made an effort to remember my birthday and make it special. I was charmed for a moment. But I'll let you in on how I *knew* he had forgotten my birthday. The next morning, I didn't receive a birthday card or flowers, and when we went out to dinner, he didn't even have reservations! It was a great thing our relationship ended before the next important date could roll around. I hate expectations, but to disregard your girlfriend's birthday and try to play it off like it was important was just heartbreaking to me. I would have rather he just admitted he forgot and saved me the pony dance.

and drive to the dealer, you are going to have to wait for hours
before your car is serviced, if they can even squeeze you in. You
can take it to a drive-through oil change station, but you aren't
going to get the attention or specialization to your make and
model that you would at the dealer. However, if you call ahead
and make an appointment at the dealer's service center, you can
walk right in and they will normally shuttle you back to work
and pick you up when your car is ready.

Isn't that nice? Instead of having to wait all day in the lounge
watching the Weather channel until your car can be serviced, if
you have an appointment, the service technicians will even greet
you by name. Doesn't that make you feel special?

Make her feel special by making dinner reservations ahead
of time. No one wants to have to wait to sit down and eat a nice
romantic dinner with you. And since it's a special occasion, don't
just ask her what she feels like eating. Don't you hate it when you
take your car to Jiffy Lube and they ask you what type of oil you
would like in your engine? They're the specialists; how should you
remember what the last guy put in your engine? They should have
it stored somewhere in the computer. It was bad enough having to
take time out of your busy day to get your oil changed. Now you
have to tell them what to put in your engine. You might as well do
it yourself. So know where your date's favorite restaurant is and take
her there, and don't forget to call ahead so you don't have to wait.

To sum this up, flowers and a card should be personalized and
sent on time, and they are not considered a gift unless you are in
a bind. A gift is something that can be unwrapped and preferably
something she would like. Some no-fail gift options include tickets
to an event, lingerie, clothing, perfume, etc. I understand that

automatically knowing what a woman likes to eat or receive can be a little hard, so it is totally okay to ask a girl her favorite food, restaurants, stores, and clothing sizes. But make sure it's part of a conversation, and don't wait to have that conversation a few days before a special occasion or she'll know something's up. These personal hints from her will make gift buying as easy as automatically knowing that your car uses 10w-30 instead of 10w-50.

Chapter 5:
Playing Under the Hood

If you opened up this book and turned straight to this chapter, raise your hand. Okay, now that we have that settled, let's get down to business. That's right; we're going to talk about sex, a very important part of relationship maintenance. So important, in fact, that it deserves its own chapter.

A QUICK LESSON ON PROTECTIVE DEVICES

Can someone please explain to me how men have no problem spending fifteen minutes to place a car cover over their priceless automobile to protect it from dust, rain, and sun damage *and* have no problem hassling with locking their steering wheel with the Club to protect it from car thieves *and* have no problem parking it blocks away from their destination so no one will park close enough to possibly ding their door, yet men still have such a problem putting a condom on to protect their health?

Guys, really, no matter what excuse you throw at a woman, the truth is that you just don't like putting one on. I had a boyfriend complain about the cost of having to supply the condoms, yet he had no problem shelling out four hundred dollars to install an alarm system that would begin to beep if someone came within a couple of feet from his car.

And who came up with the idea that the woman should be responsible for everything and just take the Pill? Cars don't automatically come with a protection plan. That is an upgrade you pay for. Even when you drive it off the lot with an alarm already installed, the dealer didn't just throw in a security system for you and say Merry Christmas! You paid for it somewhere in the breakdown. Expecting a girl to have condoms with her or to be on the Pill is unacceptable. Plus it isn't only pregnancy you need to worry about nowadays. So do me a favor and buy the economy pack of condoms at Costco, and take a moment to use them. Nothing is worth the price of risking your life or the life of your partner. If you are allergic to latex, there are latex-free condoms; the same way you cherish your car enough to go the extra mile and protect it from predators, take a moment to protect yourself from any diseases.

Also, you should feel comfortable enough to ask your partner when her last STD test was and vice versa. Don't get upset if she asks you for an STD test either. Knowledge is power and STDs are spreading at record rates because people don't know they are carriers. So take the time to get tested regularly and invest in a protection plan for your body. Girls, if you are reading this, self-advocacy is key. Don't let a man drive his car into your garage without a car cover; no one can keep your health in mind better than you. Okay, that is as serious as I will be for the rest of your read. Now that we have covered safety, let's get down to the fun stuff!

NOT EVERY MODEL HAS THE SAME ENGINE

The same way that repairs on your V8 are different than on your last car, which was a V6 or V4, keep in mind that what your last girlfriend enjoyed, your new girlfriend may not. Some cars don't even have the engine underneath the hood, they have it in the trunk! Imagine if you approached a Volkswagen buggy assuming it had the same make as a BMW—you would never even find the engine. Some women may require more time and effort to please in bed than others, but female orgasms can and do exist all the time! If a man can climax every time, there is no reason why a woman should not.

Think of it this way: in a simple attempt to tune up a V8, its engine is so big that trying to move anywhere under the hood is nearly impossible. It takes some serious patience and a good understanding of exactly where parts are and which may require special tools in order to get into the small gaps to reach your destination. Some engines are much easier. When making repairs on a V4, the engine is so small that you can get your hands in pretty much anywhere without any frustrations or struggles at all.

Unlike making repairs under the hood of your car, where all you have to guide you is a manual, working on a woman is not only more fun, it can be a lot easier because unlike your manual, women talk. All you have to do is listen and pay attention. Women will tell you what turns them on. They will also tell you what they are not into. Listen to a woman's body language. If you are having oral sex with a girl and she is pulling away from you or pushing you away by your shoulders, that's a clue! Take a break from that area for a while, and when you return, be gentler. On the other hand, if she is pushing her hips toward you, then keep going, Don Juan, you're doing something right and she wants more. If you are trying to put your lips or fingers somewhere and she moves away from you, cool your jets, Dexter, because she's just not into that. And if there's something new you'd like to try, you may want to wait until you're out of the bedroom to bring it up for the first time to avoid killing the moment if she's offended.

The best way to get to know what your woman enjoys and what she doesn't is by communication. Communicating does not only involve talking about things but listening to what she is asking of you. Some women spoil their men in bed and are very open to many different positions, new ideas, and even toys. However, this does not apply to all women. One thing that does apply to all women is that they will not all enjoy everything your last sexual partner did and that is not a bad thing unless your needs are very specific and she is just not open to trying those things. Also keep in mind how you are approaching a new suggestion. You'd be surprised how much more women open up to trying new things if you word your request properly. Some experimenting may make a woman feel dirty or scared or sinful, so be mindful and use only your best bedside manner when speaking to your girlfriend about sex. Be gentle in your approach and you may be surprised how comfortable your woman may be with you in bed.

DREAM CARS

There is nothing wrong with fantasizing about the cherry-red Corvette your neighbor is driving—as long as you never actually go to your neighbor's garage and take it out for a spin when he's not home! Catch my drift?

Studies have shown that fantasies can actually be a healthy thing in relationships as long as the person creating the fantasy can tell the difference between fantasy and reality. Sometimes you may get tired of driving your Chevy Tahoe every day and you may wish you were in the newest Escalade with all the sweet upgrades. You can see yourself enjoying the leather seats and twenty-two-inch rims, and then you remember you signed a five-year deal on the Chevy and have no choice but to continue payments on your commitment.

Playing out your fantasies with your partner is also a great way to share what's on your mind. This is also a good way to share with your partner what you would like from her in a slightly safer way than just bugging her for it, or turning to someone else to get it. So go ahead, tell her how if you were driving the Chevy you would like to take the turns a little harder and blast the radio without caring if you are disturbing the neighbors. Just remember, if you are driving a Chevy in real life and are sharing your fantasies with your partner, keep the fantasy about your driving a Chevy and not the neighbor's Corvette! In other words, use her name, not Pamela Anderson's, not Carmen Electra's, not the neighbor's, and certainly not the cute intern's at your day job.

NEVER FORCE A CAR TO START

Sometimes sex doesn't happen the way you plan it. Men tend to get frustrated with a woman when sex doesn't come right away or when a man finds himself really working hard to convince a woman to have sex. If you find yourself in a situation where you wish she would hurry up and put out, or even worse, you find yourself asking her over and over again why she won't have sex with you, there are a couple of things to keep in mind.

If she gives you an inch, don't try to take a mile. If you guys are messing around but she isn't ready to go all the way, don't push things, let her be the one who goes all the way. If she's rolling around in bed with you she is clearly attracted to you, and when she feels comfortable with the situation she will let you know. There is nothing more annoying to a woman than a guy who tries to push the issue of sex. Let her come around to it when she is ready. For some women, once you are in a relationship you are golden. For others it still takes time. Even if you are already having sex, pushing sex on a girl will get you nowhere.

Pushing for sex is like when you try to start your car and it won't start. You may turn the key in the ignition and hear a crank, but no matter how many times you crank it and no matter how much it sounds like it is *almost* going to start, the car isn't going to start. If you keep trying to force the situation by continuing to turn the key, you are going to do one of two things: burn out your starter or wear out your battery.

Should you be that guy who thinks you just might get clever by trying to pump the gas pedal between cranks to make the car start, sweetie, you are wasting your time, because if you have a fuel-injector engine you can pump it all you want but nothing is going to happen. If you have a carburetor engine, you keep pumping that gas pedal and you are going to end up flooding your engine, my friend. So back off. You are only making the situation worse by aggressively trying to make the car start.

To properly start your car, you need three elements: gas, air, and a spark. If you are missing one of the three, you are not going anywhere. The same is true with sex. If she is not ready or not in the mood, you are missing the spark, so don't force it. Sex is like getting cars to start—you need all the elements to be there: passion, romance, and a *spark*. If any element that turns a girl on is missing, pushing the issue will not make the timing any better. Sometimes timing may be the spark. Every girl requires different elements to get her in the mood, so take a moment to find out what turns her on.

Whatever her reason for not having sex with you may be, respect it. If a woman finds herself resorting to the ultimate excuse—having a headache—please stop every attempt you are making at that time. When a girl says she will not have sex because she has a headache, you have officially exhausted all options. Every woman has read in one magazine or another that sex is one of the best remedies to relieve a headache. It helps the circulation of blood to the head. So when a girl says no to sex and throws you the headache excuse, she just doesn't want to have sex with you at the moment. So back off a little without getting upset or frustrated and let it happen when the time is right.

TRANSLATING A DIAGNOSTIC TEST

Women have different needs than men do, and the language we use to express these needs has different meanings than the words of men. You have already heard me talk about how, as women, we have grown up with words like "princess." Now that I have put women into terms that are easier for you to understand, it's time for you to open yourself up more to understanding a woman and a woman's vocabulary. Trust me, it's only going to make things easier. Just like when a mechanic connects your car to a diagnostic machine when something is wrong but you can't exactly figure out what it is, the mechanic will explain what each code means by putting things in terms you can understand. I am here to translate what a woman is trying to tell you.

There's a common phrase: treat others the way you would like to be treated. But actually, you should not treat a woman the way you would like to be treated—you should treat her the way *she* wants to be treated. Everyone wants to be treated with respect and kindness, which is what the golden rule is all about. But when it comes to women, the things that make you happy are not necessarily going to be what makes her happy. As much as she might love football, she probably enjoys a night on the town just as much, and probably prefers a sparkly bracelet as a gift over a Snuggie emblazoned with the logo of her favorite NFL team.

One favorite word in a woman's vocabulary that sparks much confusion in the minds of men is "romance." What is romance to a woman? It's something that sets a mood and ambiance. Romance requires an effort on your part, inspired by the heart and mind. It can be as simple as preparing a picnic in your backyard under the stars or in the living room on a rainy night, complete with candles and soft music. Romance is seduction. It's little things that will trigger her five senses: sound, touch, smell, taste, and sight. One guy I dated thought that was easy; he interpreted this as him smelling good, looking good, tasting good, sounding good, and being able to touch me "good." I couldn't help but laugh, but this is a prime example of what a man may think of when he hears a woman asking for romance and what a woman considers romance. If you are having trouble trying to evoke those senses, think of music, body rubs, scented candles, champagne, and moonlight. Now that's romance!

One common mistake men tend to make is that they confuse romance with foreplay. Here's where you have to remember to treat a woman how *she* wants to be treated. Foreplay may be your idea of romance, but most women would beg to differ. Leaving a note on our pillow while we are in the shower getting ready for bed is romantic. It's not about getting her hot and bothered. Foreplay isn't just about some high-school-style groping before you get down to business. Don't get me wrong—we love when a man spends a little extra time warming us up—but we need something to satisfy our psychological needs as well. Remind us that we are special and worth the extra time it took to think of running us a bath, filling a vase with our favorite flowers, or just telling us how much we are appreciated. Even a sexy text during the day can start setting the tone for the night.

Why do you think chick flicks are successful? They are based on a woman's fairytale. In fact, if you're ever having a hard time coming up with a date idea or need some romantic inspiration, rent one! Some of my favorites are *Love Actually*, *Dirty Dancing*,

Sweet Home Alabama, Love and Basketball, and *The Wedding Date, Pretty Woman,* and all of J-Lo's movies tell similar stories of a woman's dream of the knight in shining armor who comes and sweeps us off our feet. Even the most modern woman loves these movies. And, as the movie goes, with romance comes sex.

Romancing your lady is like waxing your car: you are going to need to put some elbow work into it. The end result is worth bragging about. You could just wash your car and skip the wax, but the truth is you are much happier with how your car will look when you take the time to wax it. It works out any small scratches, and when it rains the dirt will just wash right off. There are many benefits to putting the extra effort into your car. And it works the same with your woman. When you go the extra mile to make your woman happy and make her feel special with a little romance, the other aspects of your relationship will benefit as well.

Chapter 6:

A Trip to the Mechanic

No matter how cool your girl may be, she is never going to be a man. She may love sports more than you do, she can be cool with you having a guys' night out whenever you want and staying out as late as you wish, but at the end of the day she is still a woman— with womanly emotions and behaviors. You can put a Corvette engine in a Camaro and your car will run and sound cool, but you are still driving a Camaro. In a relationship involving more than just casually dating, there are a few major, emotionally elevating obstacles you will face.

WHEN YOUR RADIATOR OVERHEATS

Despite all rumors to the contrary, women do not like to argue. We also don't always have to be in control or be right (well, we do like to be right).

When a couple argues, the cause and effect are similar to when a car overheats. Your car may be overheating for a variety of reasons, and whatever the reason is, it's beginning to cause a serious problem. When your car overheats, the main issue has to do with your radiator. Your problem may be a hole in a hose, a crack in the radiator, a missing fan belt (this is a big one because not only is your car going to overheat but you're probably going to blow your alternator as well), or your thermostat may be out, but any of these problems left untouched long enough will result in your radiator overheating. And all of these problems, if caught promptly, can be easily fixed without a hefty price tag. Even a bad crack in the radiator can be sealed if you catch it in time. The key is listening to your car and paying attention to all the signals it sends you before you cause other things under the hood to suffer from your negligence.

When your car starts to overheat, the signs are simple: they start off with the hot and cold idle on the gauge of your dashboard leaning more and more towards the hot side. Then the idle reaches the hot side, and if by this time you do not pull over and allow your car to cool down, soon your car is going to make you pull over when the smoke from under your hood scares you enough to believe that your car is about to blow up. Now, if you are half as smart as I hope you are, you should have started to pay attention to the problem when you first saw the sign of overheating. You could have started by turning off the air conditioner and pulling over to the side of the road to let the car begin to cool for a moment while you figured out what was causing the problem. You also could have tried to get to a gas station and put some water into the radiator to help cool the car, but you are intelligent enough to know the more you drive the car, the worse the situation is going to get. Even times people believe they can help cool their overheated car by driving with their heater on, the best thing to do is just pull over and give it time to cool off. I need to make this as clear as possible: when your car is overheating, regardless of what you think may help get you through the smoke, just stop the car and let it cool off before trying to fix it. If you try to open the cap on a smoking hot radiator, you will burn yourself with its toxic fluid. Let it cool off first.

Similar solutions apply to arguing with your lady. The key is to really try and understand what your girlfriend is so upset about, what caused her to react this way. When she is arguing with you, try to understand her motive. What is her intention with the fight that she is trying to get you understand? When you have an argument, you have most likely hurt her feelings; remember that most of the time, anger is caused by hurt. Even if you can tell me she is fighting just to fight, there is an intention behind that fight. Some people fight because when the other person fights back that shows them you still care enough to get angry. It is a terrible and unhealthy source of drama, but what is even unhealthier is that in this case, your girlfriend may be lacking attention from you.

This works both ways. Men sometimes start a fight because they also lack attention and may try to express their desires and motives in their arguments. However, in a heated moment people forget that in order to find a solution to your fight, you need to take a moment to figure out what the objective to the fight is. Some people call it emotional intelligence, and Buddhists call it compassion. Whatever you want to call it, every fight has a reason. To discover the solution, you must both learn to manage your emotions so you can identify and then assess the issue before continuing to engage in a heated battle that is only going to escalate into a bigger problem.

Sometimes men ask me why they have to do all the work to try to calm their girlfriends. I always tell them, "Many times it isn't easy, but someone needs to be the adult and try a new approach to set an example." Sorry, guys, but when you own a car, it isn't going to fix itself. As frustrating as it may sometimes get, you have to do the fixing.

CAR CONTROL

Fights are never fun, and people tend to forget that when emotions are high, intelligence is low. The saying "all is fair in love and war" is a huge problem when you are at war with someone you love. People tend to say things they don't really mean when they are angry and forget the power of words. Don't forget that once you have said something nasty, you cannot take it back. If you continue hurting each other, your relationship will only suffer. Make it a conscious decision to choose your words wisely. When you are speaking hurtfully from emotions, your lady will only do the same. Be careful not to engage in battles like these.

Knowing when to back down is important for men and women in a relationship. It is like downshifting before a sharp turn at high speeds. There is an entire mastering of the heel-toe maneuver in race-car driving that allows you to safely take a turn and still have speed. People think it is easy, and for my first year of racing cars with Mazda, I actually thought it wasn't important. But I quickly learned that if I didn't know when to back off and when it was safe to give the car throttle again, I was going to do one of two things when taking corners at high speeds: I was going to lose major speed around the turn because I was too scared to take the corner with proper speed; or I would go into a turn with so much speed and adrenaline that it might cause me to drop two tires and lose control of my car, spinning me straight into a wall. I experienced both scenarios in a race and that was when I learned how crucial it is to control my actions, even when I think I am right. As fast as I have been the leader in a race, I just as quickly shot myself in the foot and wrecked out of the race.

A car can only take so much before it loses control. The only way a car can lose control is if the person driving doesn't have control. Fighting with your loved one at a heated moment is not much different. Get the emotions under control first and then try to fix the problem.

In a relationship, emotional control is just as important as car control. Let's say she's upset because you did something wrong; whatever you did (hypothetically you are at fault this time), you hurt her feelings and she is looking for your understanding and compassion. If you even attempt to argue with your upset woman, you are going to fail drastically. She is arguing with you so you can understand what you did to hurt her, and this way you hopefully will not do it again. Trust me, no matter how much we fight with you, we know that even a screamfest can't change what you have said or done.

So although it may not feel that way at the moment, the ball is actually in your court. Take a moment to realize she is upset and hurt by your behavior. Don't battle to defend yourself; it is only going to make matters worse. You can keep a car from spinning if you keep your cool and slowly regain control of your car. So if you're about to start arguing, slow down a moment and think about the situation or about what you have done and what you can do to make sure you do not do it again. Put yourself in her shoes. Think of how you would have felt had she done or said something inconsiderate to you. You may have to swallow your pride and you may think she is overreacting, but you are not her so you don't know *exactly* how you made her feel. You may have hit a sore spot that you never knew existed. So have compassion in your arguments and take a moment to think things through before you start to say anything.

Instead of speaking to defend yourself, choose words and actions that will heal the problem. If you caused the problem, think about using words that are calming to an upset woman, like, "I understand why you would get so upset, I was very inconsiderate." This is validating her emotions, which is an instant cooler as long as the tone of your voice matches your statement. When people argue, they are arguing a point. Once their opponent has agreed with their point, there is nothing left to argue over. So the faster you understand why she is so upset with you and the faster you understand how to avoid behaving in a way that hurts her, the faster you can move on to making up (and we all know how fun that can be!)

RECKLESS DRIVING

If you are recklessly driving your brand new Ferrari down a winding road and wrap your car around a pole, you are not going to get away with telling the officer "I'm sorry." Trying to use your circumstances as an excuse isn't going to work either; in fact, it may just make it worse. "I'm sorry, officer, but I was drunk. Otherwise, I never would have been speeding or driving recklessly." That is the *last* thing that is going to get you out of your mistake.

Now of course everyone makes mistakes, and mistakes are there to learn from, and in most cases, as long as we never repeat them, they are forgivable. Let's take another look at that car wreck. The truth is that as long as you came out of the catastrophe alive, you are going to be okay. You might spend a night in jail, have to pay a ton of money in fines and damages, and your car may never run the same, but as long as you're alive, you are going to be okay. It's going to cost you dearly in other ways too: physically you are going to be sore, emotionally you will be stressed, and as I mentioned, financially almost broke. "I'm sorry" isn't going to do anything for that.

It's time to accept responsibility for your actions. After a certain age you should know the difference between right and wrong, which makes "I'm sorry," in some cases, unmoving. "I'm sorry" has sadly become the biggest misused phrase in the English language. You know that the outcome of getting caught doing something you shouldn't be doing can cause hurt to someone else, so you can't really genuinely be sorry about it.

Let's go back to that Ferrari tragedy. You know that driving down a winding road at an unsafe speed can get you a ticket, cause an accident, and cause physical harm to yourself and others. So if you do something knowing you really shouldn't be doing it, "I'm sorry" doesn't cut it, because you knew beforehand the potential harm you could have caused. You may regret your actions, but that's not the same thing. Especially because had you not gotten caught, regret and remorse would not be an emotion in your vocabulary.

Women like to hear the words of apology come out of your mouth when you do something wrong, but words won't fix what you did. Admitting to a woman that you were wrong for what you did is important. We feel better when you acknowledge that you hurt us, but we also want to know that you aren't going to do it again. Some women may not be able to forgive your mistake, and that is understandable. That is another risk you take when you make a mistake; you may risk losing the person you hurt.

So what do you do to show remorse for what you've done? Just like with the Ferrari example, you are going to have to work a little to let her know this isn't something you are going to make a habit. Apologizing is only the beginning. Following up on the apology is the next step. Flowers are always nice but they do not change what you have done.

NOTE FROM THE PASSENGER SEAT

I once dated a man who knew no boundaries. This man felt that whatever trouble he got himself into, he would find a way to charm his way out of it. He messed up in our relationship time after time. So I told him I didn't want to hear any more apologies and the flowers only left a mess when they died, so from now on "I'm sorry" had better come in a little blue box (as in from Tiffany & Co!). The next time he messed up (we're only human), he went to our jeweler and bought me a gorgeous, flawless, half-carat diamond ring in the shape of a flower. When he gave it to me, he told me that this time the flower would never wilt, and I would never have to clean up after his mess again.

That ring cost him so much money that he never again wanted to have to apologize in that manner. I was so overwhelmed with the fact that he really heard me and wanted to show me he was making an effort that I almost didn't care about the ring. Though I certainly appreciated it, the words expressing to me that he realized how much he'd been hurting me and was going to change his behavior meant much more to me than the ring. We continued to date for a long time, and he never put himself in a position where he would have to apologize again, because he genuinely felt bad for hurting my feelings and wanted to be a better man.

*   *   *

The best way to ask for forgiveness isn't with words, and no matter how nice a gift is, it won't show a girl you feel so bad for whatever you did that you are not going to do it again. The best way to ask for forgiveness is to prove it with your actions. Show that you feel so awful for what you did that you would never hurt that person again. As I said before, everyone makes mistakes. Unfortunately, this means I have more than one personal experience to share with you in this category, but here's one.

I once dated a man whom I loved more than I had ever loved anyone. After we had been dating for three years, he had a six-month affair with his best friend. When I found out, I felt so betrayed and disrespected by both of them that I decided to end the relationship.

I have never had anyone beg for my forgiveness like this man did. He would do anything, *anything* for me to return to him. He swore he had learned from his mistake, and it would never happen again. After some time, I decided to give him a second chance. He still wanted to continue to have a close friendship with the woman he had had the affair with, and to me that was a slap in the face. I felt that if he was really that sorry, he would have terminated that friendship to make sure they would never find themselves facing any kind of temptation again. I hated making him feel like he had to choose between me and his best friend, but to me, she was just a reminder of how he had lied to me for six months. It wasn't until he understood that I wasn't trying to be controlling of his friends but that I was trying to forget the pain they both caused me that he realized how continuing to see her would never allow me to heal from their mistake.

My stomach would turn every time she would call or try to hang out with him. It wasn't until he completely eliminated her from his life and *showed* me he was so sorry for what he had done, that he would end a friendship with this woman to put my feelings first, that I was able to move past what he had done and be comfortable in our relationship again.

Forgiving is a very hard thing to do sometimes, and it's important to understand that it is okay to forgive as long as you are going to be able to drop the situation. I once dated a man who taught me a "1, 2, 3, over it" technique. When something would come up, we would work through it until I felt my feelings were validated and he understood that he couldn't behave in a manner that would hurt me, or vice versa. He'd count to three and we'd both say "over it" at the same time. It sounds silly and childish, but the logic behind it was that if both of us weren't truly over it yet, we wouldn't say "over it" until we were happy with the resolution. Once I felt my feelings were validated and he truly felt remorse for his actions to where he would never do it again, I'd say "over it," and since I truly was over it I would never bring it up again.

Mistakes can strain a relationship, and most of the time you really have to put in an effort to make things right. But if you go back to comparing your mistake to wrecking your car, most of the time it is repairable if you give it the proper care. Going the distance to take it to the dealership may cost you more and they may find more problems than you knew you had, but if you take it to any old body shop and just Band-Aid it up, you are only pacifying the situation until the car can't take it anymore. Then it may just break down, leaving you high and dry. The right thing to do is repair your car at any cost and put forward the same effort into showing your lady you will not make the same mistake again.

WHEN THE CAR STOPS RUNNING

In the same way that it's a given that mistakes are made, there will come a time that you will realize the party is over. That is unless you're head over heels and ready to commit. In that case, move on to the next chapter, big boy! But if you find yourself at the end of the road, there are two ways you get there. Either she calls it off with you or you call it off with her. Now for the most part, women are very gentle and hate causing hurt to anyone— well … unless you piss them off. And if that is what's causing her to call it off, I don't feel bad for you, and frankly, you deserve every last object she is throwing at you while telling you to get out. Let's spend some time considering the other potential endings to a relationship and the best way to handle each situation.

She's Ready to Get Rid of the Old Thing If she is secure in her decision to leave, even if you aren't ready to let her go, do not try to convince her to stay. Have you ever driven a car up a hill on a hot day in the desert when the gas light is already on? Just the thought of it is painful. Your car may try with everything it's got to get through that rough spot and get you to the top of the hill—it will huff and puff and rattle and grind but the truth is, no matter how much you encourage your car to make it up that hill on its last drops of gas, you aren't going to make it. Even if you insist to the point that you try to push your car up the hill, you will only exhaust yourself and feel even worse because you tried so hard and now you have failed.

When a woman is ready to leave, she is ready. Women are not like men, where a good romp or a guilt trip might make her stick around a little longer. When a woman has given the relationship all she has, she will use that last gallon in her tank to recoup and start over by getting away from you and healing herself. If she is leaving because she has found someone else, pushing her to stay with you will only result in her becoming annoyed and realizing that the other guy is more easygoing and not as pushy. You cannot convince her to stay. It is hard for a woman to move on when she has been with a man for a long time—and sometimes even eight months is a long time for us.

A woman will be the first to try and make a relationship work. I once knew a woman who was willing to try sending her hyper child to boarding school in order to convince her boyfriend to stay with her! Women will try everything before letting go, but when they are ready to let the book close, it will be shut, locked, and stored away. She will not try to call you or even run into you. I moved fifteen hundred miles once to forget about a man. But before I was ready to leave him, I tried everything to save our relationship. I read books, followed a therapist's advice, his mother's advice; I tried it all. By the time he was ready to work things out, it was too late. (Sort of like what I mentioned earlier. By the time you realize something's wrong, it has probably been on her mind for some time, so pay attention to the signals she is sending before you end up in this situation!) When he was finally ready, I was over him, and I had a new life fifteen hundred miles away that no longer included him.

So the day you get the talk that things just aren't the same anymore, or she loves you but isn't "in love" with you anymore, ask her if there is anything you can do to light the spark again. If she says, "No, I wish there was but there isn't," accept it. You can tell her you will always be a phone call away if she ever needs you and you love her and will never forget every wonderful moment with her. You can tell her you will miss her and you will always be there for her, but let her go. You had some good times together so there's no reason not to end things amicably. If she uses the word "No" in her response, your next step is to peacefully let her go.

Now if she answers with something like, "I don't know, I am just confused right now," you can proceed to do whatever you can to try to win her back because the book isn't fully shut. She may still be harboring hope that one day you will be the man that treats her better than his stupid car and will somehow, in an unexplainable way, just wake up and be the man that she has been wanting for so long. But don't deceive her. Only be the man that you can be 100 percent of the time. There's no point in wooing her back with false promises because you'll end up in this spot again soon enough.

A quick side note: if your girlfriend is so upset that she is throwing your stuff all over the apartment, it's time to realize how far over you she is and leave quickly before you take a shoe to the forehead. Have your buddy pick up your crap in the morning, and count your blessing that you got out of that battlefield alive. Whatever you did was serious, and you will not be forgiven.

OBO (Or Better Offer) Look, let's be honest here: when a man leaves a woman, it is normally because he has found another woman who is more appealing to him. A man will not give up a steady play-date for no reason. He may not be that into a girl but will stick around if it means getting laid three times a week. So when you are giving her the talk, be kind to her, and whatever you do, don't lead her on. Be honest. If you are leaving her because you found someone else and it is becoming too much of a hassle keeping their names straight, just say it. She will use the anger and hurt as fuel to get over you that much quicker.

Saying you'd like to remain friends only makes it harder on her, regardless of how much you might mean it. Right now, just let her down honestly but softly. Think of it as if you have just gotten a new car and your old car wasn't worth trading in so you decided to just sell it to a private party. Even though you may be driving your new car all around town, you still wash your old car and fix up any major problems, at least to make it appealing for another buyer. You still put some love into it before you tape the for-sale sign on it. You could eventually get tired of trying to sell the car and donate it for a tax write-off, but you would never just take the car to a junkyard and toss it when it still runs perfectly fine. It has taken you everywhere you have needed while you two shared your time together, so have the decency to still be kind to it even though it is now part of your past.

If you are coming to the end of the road with your girlfriend, take the same approach. Always be kind—if not for the sake of not wanting to cause her pain, then for the sake of treating others the way you would like to be treated. Who knows, one day your newer model might just leave your butt high and dry, stranded with nowhere to go. Be considerate with her feelings and expect that she may cry. (We *are* women, we do that.) As much as she is hurting, cut the cord and don't string her along out of guilt. She may hate you because you broke her heart, but she will still have respect for you.

One common phrase men use when ending a relationship is, "It's not you, it's me." Of course it isn't her! It is you who wants to end things, not her. Women *hate* to hear this. It doesn't make our feelings hurt any less. So let's take one small step for mankind and eliminate that phrase from your vocabulary.

If you are calling it quits because you just aren't feeling it anymore, you may want to still try and date, just not as seriously. But understand that it is very hard to take a demotion in a relationship, and you may run into problems down the road where she will start to question you on your whereabouts when you don't spend every night with her. Understand that she is used to spending much of her time with you and most nights with you. Becoming a casual dating partner or "friends with benefits" may not work as smoothly as you would like. Regardless of how you choose to end the relationship, whether by just a clean break or trying to let it dwindle away, always keep one thing in mind—kindness.

ENGAGING YOUR ANTILOCK BREAKING SYSTEM—ABS

Have you ever been on a winding road and felt like your control of the car was so great that you were taking all the curves well above the recommended speed limit? Like a racecar driver with your hands perfectly positioned on the wheel and your body straight and tight, your shoulders are back, and you are just zooming through the winding turns until, suddenly, you hit a sharper-than-expected turn that sends your right foot right to the brake in a serious panic. The panic ends the fun and you realize you were going way too fast and could have wrapped yourself around a pole. You quickly return to driving but with caution, paying attention to your surroundings. The truth is, you suddenly hit reality and realized you're not Jeff Gordon, speed racer. Sometimes you may be going so fast you don't even realize the speed at which you are moving until something in the road freaks you out so badly, you hit the brakes hard enough to feel the wonders of your ABS (antilock braking system). You will know when this happens because your car actually jumps as your tires lock up, and any forward movement causes serious tire smoke, and you are typically left with that "oh crap that was close" feeling.

Sometimes a relationship can produce the very same feeling, in a similar pattern. Plenty of people get so caught up in the intensity of their relationship that before they know it, they feel pressure to move faster to the next step. Suddenly you realize you aren't really as ready as you thought you were and you get frightened. It's a scary feeling, but it's not the end of the world. The best thing to do is to be honest with your partner and tell her that things are moving faster than you can handle. Honesty is key in all aspects of a relationship. And trust me, she would rather have you ask her to slow things down now than find herself with a guy who feels trapped or obligated further down the road.

It is easy to get caught up in something that feels right, especially if you are having fun in a new relationship. Girls love it! Sometimes it feels like stealing the car without sounding off the alarm. Before you realize it, you are in a relationship and did not even know it. You were so caught up that you had no idea all her stuff was already at your house, until one day reality sets in and you wonder why she has spent two full weeks at your house without needing to go home to get a change of clothes.

We all get caught up in things, and we all wake up to reality and get a little freaked out by it when things have moved too fast. It's perfectly fine and normal to take a deep breath and slow down, as long as you are honest and tell a girl things are moving too fast. She may not understand what you mean, so explain to her that you still want to date her, you just want to take your time getting to know each other. Just like when you are driving too fast and you hit the brakes so hard you engage your ABS, you still continue to drive but you drive a little slower. So if you are one to freak out, don't be so quick to end the relationship. Sometimes your relationship isn't over, you may just need to slow things down.

Chapter 7:
Permanent Parking

When buying a new car, there comes a point when the car salesman will sit you down at the negotiation table. His main objective is to get you to commit to one of the cars you test drove. He will change his entire demeanor. Now he is all business and will push and push, giving you so many different ways to justify going over your budget by working in rebates and telling you that this car was made for you and only you—whatever it will take for him to seal the deal. And it will be at that point, at that very table, that you will need to decide: do you sign on the dotted line and take the car, or do you walk away and hope you can find a new car lot somewhere within a fifty-mile radius you haven't hit up yet, and test drive a little more?

Whatever you decide to do at that moment is up to you, but the real point is that once you are at the negotiation table, you have to make a decision. The car salesman is telling you to buy or get off his lot.

It's a tactic women use too. There will come a day that the standard boyfriend/girlfriend situation just isn't cutting it anymore. Our negotiation table is when we give you the ultimatum to move forward with us or move out. The ball's in your court, you can do what you want with it. You can either ruin a great deal or take what you have chosen and make something really great out of it, but it is time to start taking the future into perspective.

BUY OR GET OFF THE LOT

All right, Casanova, now's the time to be truthful with yourself. There is going to be a point in your life that if you decide you want to have a family one day, you are going to have to start to make some commitments and changes in your life. I am not here to prepare you for all the life changes you will need to make to get you there (or we would be here for a *very* long time!), but I am here to make you realize that if you want to have a family, the first step toward that is monogamy and long-term commitment—and having a girlfriend for five years is pushing the issue.

A woman is going to start having the "engagement itch" between the two- and three-year mark. Depending on her age, her feelings toward marriage may differ, but it is typical for a woman to start thinking about the future around this time. At two years she will start to ask where the relationship is going and may even think about taking a break to give you that extra push, but it is between the second and third year that it will really start to linger in her mind. This will be an issue for a woman for the first couple of years, but after about the fifth year, if you two still aren't married or engaged, she will either be over the marriage fantasy altogether and be happy to have a wonderful relationship, forgetting about the timeline she has had mapped out for herself since she was twelve, or she will dump your commitment-phobic butt for a man who will turn around and put a ring on her finger after six months.

I hate to break it to you, cowboy, but there is going to be a point where she will give you an ultimatum. She shouldn't have to if you have been together this long. This should automatically be a topic that deserves a serious conversation. When you lease a car, you lease it for three years, and at the end of those three years you know you will have to make a decision. At the end of your contract you will be in a position where you have to make a choice whether to keep the car, refinance the remaining balance and purchase the car for good, or return it and move on.

Whatever you decide to do is okay, but I guarantee you that Ford isn't going to let you just go month-to-month on your car after the lease is up. Sorry, buddy, but you have to make an adult decision to either let the car go or make a commitment to keep it. But you can't keep things stagnant forever.

You should look at relationships in the same light. You can test drive the relationship, take it for a good three-year spin, but after that you should be a big boy and either buy or get off the lot. In chapter 1, we spent time figuring out what you wanted in a woman. Now it's time to evaluate whether you are satisfied with your relationship. Two to three years is a reasonable time to allow yourself to know if this is the woman you want to spend the rest of your life with. Now I am not saying that you need to marry the girl after the three years, but if you can't put an engagement ring on her finger after three years, there is probably a problem. If you are capable of making that kind of decision with a car after three years, you are capable of giving your girlfriend that same type of courtesy.

If you realize you do not see yourself spending the rest of your life with her but are comfortable and content with the way things are, tell her so she can make that choice for herself. Let her decide if she wants to continue to spend time with you without a long-term commitment, or if she would prefer to move on if she doesn't feel that the relationship is going any further. If you decide to get off the lot, remember to pay attention to being kind and considerate toward her feelings.

If you decide to take the relationship to the next step, your courage is to be admired. Keep on reading.

MEETING THE SELLERS—AKA THE PARENTS

Have you ever owned a car that was really emotionally hard to let go of? Maybe it was your very first car, or the classic car your dad had for years before handing over the keys when you turned sixteen. Maybe it was a regular old car that you just had so many memories in. I had one like this. I wrecked it so many times that I even wrecked it twice in the same day. This was the same Dodge Colt that everyone in my high school gave me grief about. But it was still my "hooptie." People that get back in contact with me from high school even ask if I still own it. Man, that car was a stallion!

As much as everyone laughed at the screws and duct tape that held it together, everyone had some kind of special memory that was made in my car. One of my friends sat in my car in the school parking lot getting drunk and ended up passing out. I went to my car to leave for lunch and found her passed out in the back seat. Another friend borrowed it for a date and lost her virginity in that car (I know, I'm a good friend!). I learned to drive with that car. I would sneak out and drive to all the big parties in that car.

I remember the first time I checked my oil. I was at a gas station, and it was late at night. My oil level was fine, but I had a hard time finding the hole that the dipstick went back into, so I put it in my backseat and drove off. My car smelled like burnt oil for days and was constantly smoking until a security guard where I worked became so concerned with my smoky car that he pointed out the obvious problem. I assured him everything was fine and it was just the oil burning on the hot engine—no big deal. I told him how I had trouble finding the hole and just threw the stick in my back seat. I will never forget the look on his face when he yelled, "Pilar, you are going to blow your engine! Give me the stick. I'll put it back in, and I'll be back with some oil to replace all the oil you have spilt!" I had no idea I had caused such a problem, and luckily it didn't turn into a very expensive lesson for me.

Every time I think of that car, I laugh. I can't help it! All the memories I have created, all the stories I can tell. All the stories my friends can tell. I was always taking the car into the school's auto shop to screw in a busted-up fender or weld a hole in my transmission pan when I ran over a curb and put a hole in it. It was because of my emotional attachment that I couldn't sell the car, even after I bought a new car. I wanted to sell it, and I told my mom I would so she would stop complaining about it sitting in our front yard for a year. But I never really put a for-sale sign on it. Finally my mom put one up for me.

People started calling to make appointments to come see the car, and if they got an appointment, they were lucky. If I didn't like the way they sounded over the phone, or if I got any impression that they were going to take it to the chop shop and sell it for parts, I would give them the wrong address or would invent something drastically wrong with the car to make them lose interest. I made it so impossible for anyone to want to buy my hooptie that my mother was the one who sold it for me. Without even telling me! For five hundred dollars! I was devastated, but she was right. I was never going to think anyone was worthy of owning my car.

This happens to many of us, even girls. I bet you can remember a car and start to smile and laugh about the memories that come to mind. I once dated a guy, and every date we went on, we would come home in a tow truck because of his little red Camaro. It left us stranded every time we would go out, but he still held on to

"Gretchen" (that's what he called it). When we came to the end of our road, I was pretty jealous of how quickly I could be replaced while he still mourned the loss of Gretchen.

It's an attachment like the one parents have to their little girl. I don't care if she is thirty years old and supporting herself, to her parents she is still their little girl. And no one will be able to provide and care for her the way they have for all those years. They want to feel comfortable that whomever they give their blessing to will be able to love her and provide for her and treat her like the rare classic car that she is. So unless you want your future mother-in-law to scare you away (like I would scare away every single buyer I had for my car), be on your best behavior! You're going to have to prove yourself to her parents. Let them see that you too see their precious daughter as the most valuable item on Earth. Be extra attentive to her when you are around her parents and make sure you are attentive to her parents as well. This will gain you points with not only her parents but with your girlfriend/fiancé as well. She is just as nervous as you and wants her parents to like you as much as she does, so even though it seems to be a given, be on your best behavior.

With that in mind, a few things on the "no-no" list while meeting her parents: do not talk about your sex life around them, do not grab her butt or put your hand on her thigh if you are sitting next to her (no matter how much you think no one will notice, they will), and if you are staying at their house, for goodness sake, don't try to sleep in her room. No matter how cute or fun the idea might seem in your head, she probably still has childhood toys in her closet, and her bed is probably so old that if you don't break it, you are at least going to hear it squeak. Getting busted for one night is not worth a lifetime of in-laws who feel they were disrespected.

Carry yourself like the classy gentleman who attracted their daughter to you in the first place, and they will be happy to have found someone who will be able to provide for their daughter, not feel like you will be a second child to support.

STAGING THE CAR SHOW

Maybe at this moment planning a wedding isn't on your immediate agenda; however, if a wedding is ever in your future, let me help you get into a woman's head on this matter. A woman's wedding day is her very own car show. And it really is *her* wedding day. Boys don't have every detail of their wedding planned out since the age of twelve. Boys don't already know what colors they want featured in their wedding when they decide to get married. Before your fiancé showed you her favorite wedding gowns in a bridal magazine, you didn't even *know* they had bridal magazines and expos. By the time a girl starts to plan her actual wedding, she already has several color schemes in mind, she has already seen several dresses that she has dreamt about, and she may even have a location planned out without you knowing it. This day is the day that every little girl has dreamt about for years. She wants everything to be perfect so it meets all of her expectations about the biggest day of her life.

Therein lies the problem, as we have a predetermined expectation of what we want this day to be. When there are expectations, there is room for disappointment. I hate expectations for this very reason alone. If everyone lived a life without expectations, disappointment would never exist. I hate to break it to you, but pretty much every woman has expectations about her wedding day.

By giving your fiancé the wedding she wants, you hope to ensure that she will give you the marriage you want. For this one day in your life, spare no expense—let her produce the best car show ever. Let the fairytale come true for her; let her have the perfect wedding where nothing goes wrong, and at the end of it all, she will get to dance with her prince charming. Now all this Disney fairytale talk may not make any sense to you, but it's about to.

Frequently, guys express their confusion about why a girl makes such a big deal about her wedding day: why she takes weeks of spa days getting her nails done or having a hairstylist do a practice run of the hairdo she will wear days before her wedding day.

Pretend you are entering your car in a show. Now you really want your car to shine and look its best. You know that you are going to need to get the car detailed. There is a big difference in price between a normal wash and a full inside-and-out detail. That's for special occasions, like this one. For your car's big day, of course you are going to go all-out and spare no expense. After all, it's not like you enter your car in shows all the time—this is a big deal. In the detail, they shampoo the seats and carpet. They wax, polish, and shine—you name it, they do it. All you do is drop it off, let them do everything they need to do, and you come back, pay the bill, and drive off to enjoy the work that has been done on your baby. You don't bitch about the price. You don't ask whether they can skip the hand wax and substitute a spray wax for a cheaper price. No, you just let them detail your car the way it should be. It's like taking your car to a day spa. And of course your car deserves it. It's not like you take your car in for a detail every time, so for such a big occasion, it is okay to splurge on your car. I mean, hey, your car has a big day coming up!

Back to the wedding. You are only going to have to splurge on it once if you play your cards right. So if she wants fresh flowers don't tell her to use silk—we know silk means "fake." If she wants two cakes—one for the two of you and one for everyone else—let her have as many cakes as she wants and don't suggest substituting them for cupcakes so everyone can have their own. And don't let me hear that you even *thought* of suggesting she bake the cake for the two of you because it would make the cake more special if she added her love to the batter. We can see right through your suggestions. They are a way to save money! We get it!

My last piece of advice on this subject is another simple truth: women look at the size of the rock on each other's hands. Even if size doesn't matter to us, we will still admire a nice rock when we see one. So the same way you didn't hold back spending an entire paycheck on upgrading your rims from stock to premium, be sure you upgrade her rock from cubic zirconium to the real deal. I'm not implying that you must have an expensive ring or wedding because it's more about the effort that you put into everything. It will mean more to us if we know you had to save up to get us a ring. So if you splurge on your car, why not on your future wife? Think of it this way: if your bride is happy, your happy ending is guaranteed!

The details surrounding your wedding will never be forgotten. I have a friend whose high school sweetheart didn't take her to prom because he decided to install a high-performance clutch in his car. To him that was more important than spending some dough on a limo and a tux. My friend still talks about it to this day, and her prom was fifteen years ago! Can you imagine if he had ruined her wedding?

WHEN THE REPAIRS START TO PILE UP

Now that you made it through the wedding and are married or at least realize you are in it for the long run, fighting is going to come more naturally. Issues like money and kids are bound to cause stress, as are general relationship problems you have accumulated over the years. It is like when you chose to buy your car when the lease was up. After you purchased the car, the more you drove it the more kinks you began to notice, and then the kinks started to turn into major unavoidable, expensive problems. And now it's on you to fix them because your car is no longer under warranty.

For example, if you own a car for ten years and you drive it back and forth to work and every other place in between, you may have a couple of fender benders here and there but you get them fixed and everything is fine. Then you start to realize that your gears just aren't shifting as smoothly. Since you have made the choice to stick with your car, you know that trading it in for a newer model would cost you more than what it would to rebuild the transmission. So you put in the time and money to take care of the car. You still love it and understand that it takes effort to keep things running smoothly. After so many years of lugging you around everywhere you have needed to go, you give that respect to the car since you love it so much.

It works out the same with your spouse. Sure you will argue, and money may get tight here and there, and kids might break an arm when your insurance policy wasn't up-to-date, but you stick by your wife and your family through thick and thin. Financial problems will cause a lot of stress on a relationship, and if you have a financial problem, like a ton of relationships do, you find yourself fighting over the dumb little things that really aren't worth the fight just because you are under so much stress over money. After so many little fights, people start to lose faith in their marriages and start to consider divorce.

But you acquired the debt and the children that helped add to that debt *together,* and the reason why you are fighting over all the small stuff is because you are irritated and worried over not having enough money to cover all the bills and necessities. Realize that *that* is the main problem, and work through it. Even people who have a good amount of money feel like they don't have enough—no amount of money feels like it is enough money for all you want to do in life.

So if you start to realize that you are fighting over things that are pointless, remember the old saying: don't sweat the small stuff.

Pick your battles for when you really need to hash things out with one another. Other than that, remember that this is your spouse, and even though there will be times you may not like her as much as you did when you first met, she will always have your back—even when you have it turned to the wall. Do not go off and trade in your car that you loved enough to purchase in the first place just because something that is expected to go out after a while needs to be repaired. Even if you buy a new car because you don't feel it's worth dropping any more money into an old one, guess what? Ten years down the road with your new car, you are going to run into the same problems. You can't keep trading them in every time there is a problem, and that advice goes for cars *and* women.

BLOWING YOUR HEAD GASKET

Once you are married, all the other tips remain the same—you still need to open doors, date your wife, never rush her, and pick your battles. What does change is regarding infidelity. When you are married and you cheat on your wife, she will be quick to find herself a new man—oh yeah, and real quick. In fact, she will run to this man so quickly, before you even knew she was divorcing your cheating self. And by the time you do find out, this man has already secured for her the house, bank account, and your paychecks for the next eighteen years of your newborn child's life.

This nice man that she's finding so much comfort and consolation in is called a lawyer. This is nothing like when she let you get away with a meaningless fling while you guys were just dating. See, cheating on your girlfriend falls under the "I'm-sorry"-won't-get-your–car-unwrapped-from-the-pole section of this book—cheating on your wife is a whole other issue.

Cheating on your wife is like blowing a head gasket—which can also lead to blowing the motor. Without a motor, your car is completely useless. A blown motor is normally caused by something as simple as forgetting to put oil in your engine. Much like forgetting that you had a wife before you had an affair. Oops. A blown motor can also be caused by just being stupid and knowing your engine is out of oil because your oil light is glowing on your dashboard. Yet you just choose to ignore the fact that you need oil. Very similar to when you know you have a wife because you are wearing a wedding band but choose to ignore the fact that you are supposed to be monogamous and faithful and loyal and all those other things you vowed when you married her and still choose to cheat. If you think you need oil but aren't sure because your oil light isn't on, check your dipstick. If you forget you have a wife or the alcohol is making you uncertain, check your ring finger (and control your dipstick).

Many times ruining your motor begins with an avoidable issue like a blown head gasket. A blown head gasket can be caused because you simply let you car over heat for too long. Then, if you do not realize your head gasket is blown or neglect to correct the problem, a blown head gasket will soon blow out your motor as well. Truthfully if you blow your head gasket you are going to feel like an idiot, because such a small act of stupidity will potentially cause you to ruin your car. All you had to do was always keep the car cool by stopping immediately when it starts to overheat and this would never have happened. Just like knowing you should have stopped yourself immediately when the temptation of cheating on your wife first crossed your mind. But you didn't do that and now you realize you screwed up. If you think by putting some coolant in the radiator at the last minute that the head gasket will not know it overheated for so long, and you will get lucky this time and never let it happen again, check the oil lid. If when you remove the oil lid you see a white milky film on it, guess what? You blew it. This isn't only an indication that you blew your head gasket, but your mistake has also blown your motor as well. That milky film is your coolant and oil mixed together which turns into an acid and basically causes everything to self-destruct. Brace yourself for a loud noise in your engine because driving with a blown head gasket is typically going to lead you to a blown engine.

So if you think that maybe your wife may not know about your off-road driving, and that if you stop right now and never do it again and she will never find out, check your credit card records. If a hotel room is charged on there, guess what? She knows. If a woman's department store charge is on there and she hasn't received surprises from you equaling that exact amount from that exact store all on the same day, she knows. Even if you just charged so much as a casual dinner that was abnormally higher than a meal for one—or at a romantic restaurant—trust me, she knows. If you are done playing stupid and are ready to accept the consequences, let's get on with laying out your next steps.

Blowing your engine by cause of pushing a problem like an already blown head gasket, means having to replace your entire engine. This is not going to be cheap, even if you hang out at a pick-and-pull junkyard and wait for a car that has your same engine in a usable condition. This is an issue so big that you may even consider donating the car for a tax write-off because you couldn't pay a dealership to take the trade. You are faced with a serious decision. Do you fix the car and consider it an expensive lesson learned, never to be repeated, or do you just let the car go and start fresh with a new car, even if you don't really want another car payment? In many cases, your mistake was so bad that it may be in your best interest to get rid of the car altogether.

When you blow your engine you can spend the money to get it fixed, but your real problem is that you have also ruined a number of items under the hood. You may not know it instantly but it will only be a matter of time before everything else under the hood starts to fall apart. You can try to fix it one by one as the problems start to occur, but the truth is you may not be able to keep up with all of the damage you have caused. You ruined the foundation of your car because of your irresponsibility, and now the whole car may suffer. No matter what you try to do, your car may have just given up.

The same applies to trying to save your marriage or long-term relationship after you have cheated. You can see a marriage counselor, and you can keep yourself on the tightest leash, letting her know where you are at all times, who you are with, and what you are doing, and there will still be a trust issue. Trust is the one thing you do not want to ruin because it is the hardest thing to regain. Sometimes it is completely impossible. Once you have cheated on your wife, even if she decides to stand by her man and work through it and you both have faith that everything will work out in the end, regaining trust may be harder than you think. No matter how strong your wife may be, she will never forget what you did, and the only way to make your marriage work after infidelity is if she is able to pretty much forget what you did.

And you too will have to forgive yourself if you are carrying the guilt with you, and if you are not, you need to realize what you did was wrong and has hurt a person you love and feel badly enough not to do it again. Until you realize in your heart that what you did was wrong, you are capable of cheating again. It is okay to forgive a person for cheating, but you have to have the strength not to bring it up and continuously punish your partner for their mistake over and over again. Every time you make a mistake, she may hold what you did over your head. It is unfortunate but normal.

Take into consideration what you did. If you try to save the marriage, your wife is going to try her hardest to block out all the thoughts that are replaying in her mind of her husband making love to another woman. She may try to keep her mouth shut when she wants to find answers to her questions. She will most likely cry in private and be there for you when you need her. If you have a wife who is willing to do that, you have an amazing woman, and that is the kind of woman you want on your team. I strongly believe that time will heal all wounds, but the healing process can be extremely difficult. So be responsible, and hopefully you won't put yourself in the situation to find out just how good a woman she is.

Chapter 8:
Manual Overload

— — — — — — — — — — — — —

At the end of the day you will learn through your own trials and tribulations that relationships come down to four things: respect, communication, compassion, and love.

You will learn that respecting and honoring your partner's feelings will keep you out of trouble. When you respect your partner, you tend to think about the repercussions of your actions before you do them and about how your behavior will impact the one you love.

Communication will help you grow with your partner. Men and women need to tell one another what they want and what they don't want. If you never tell your partner what is important to you in a relationship, big or small, how can that person ever fulfill that need? And if you never express to your partner what hurts you, how is your partner supposed to know not to behave that way? When you are communicating with your partner, remember to communicate with respect. Listen to what your partner is trying to tell you. Communicating will require honesty, so if you feel that even with open communication you are finding the need to lie to your better half for whatever reason, you are wasting each other's time. Lying is not communication. It's a waste of words for the person lying and a waste of time for the person listening to the lie.

Compassion helps you put yourself in another person's shoes. If you learn to be compassionate, you will learn to take your partner's feelings into consideration. You will learn to be gentle with her feelings and see things from her perspective, not just yours. Having and showing compassion can help you avoid arguments because you will find it pretty hard to be selfish if you are being compassionate.

Lastly and most importantly, love. Love heals all, love brings compassion, love gives you the strength to understand and forgive, and most of all, love gives you a reason to keep putting up with all the drama a relationship can have at times. If you didn't love a person, then losing him or her wouldn't matter, and the pain of forgiving him or her wouldn't hurt. If you don't love or care for a person, he or she really doesn't have the ability to hurt you. You wouldn't care what the person did if you didn't love them. Love will keep a relationship together even when both people know it's over. Love gives couples hope that one day everything will be the way it was in the beginning. Sometimes love is all it takes to fix the relationship, because love will keep you two fighting for the relationship.

Just be sure to distinguish between love and comfort. Do not stay with someone just because it is comfortable to do so. Staying with someone out of comfort is just as bad as driving an old beat-up car on its last limb cross-country. You may be comfortable not having to pay any extra money for a rental car, but this is a bad idea. You will suffer and stall in every state at least once with your hooptie.

*   *   *

I hope you feel you now have a better understanding of women. We are not impossible to understand, and it is not impossible to please us. We really are a lot like cars. Fuel us, wax us, and maintain our emotional needs, and we will let you drive us all you want.

Remember this when you're overwhelmed with your relationship; when you first open the hood of your car it can be overwhelming. When all you want to do is add oil and you see hoses, fan belts, radiators, distributor caps, plugs, sparks, shocks, struts, engines, batteries, and multiple caps to open, it can seem intimidating. But if you just take a step back and relax before you start opening caps and pulling plugs, you can maintain your focus on one piece at a time. You will learn that even though everything in one way or another is connected to the engine, you'll notice what each part is directly connected to and what its function is. I promise that you won't be lost, and you will be able to open the hood and know that to the right is the battery and to the front is the radiator. With some time and effort, it will become almost like a map, and you will know what the problem is and exactly where you need to look to fix it.

Women and relationships can be seen the same way. We have emotions and outbursts, and some days you may feel we came from an entirely different planet, but no matter what the problem may be, it all connects to the heart. Actions are triggered by emotions, good and bad, and emotions are felt by the heart. If the mind is telling the body to react a certain way, it is because something is going on in the heart. When you get a wonderful reaction from someone, you should take a moment to realize what triggered that so you can trigger it again. You always want to keep the heart flowing properly to keep the relationship healthy and happy.

And for those of you who wonder why I never touched on the men who own an entire harem of cars, well, I will leave you with this: if you can financially afford to keep up with maintenance, registration, and insurance, as well as providing a safe parking lot for multiple vehicles, then be my guest. While Hugh Hefner may not have kept a wife, he sure did master the art of keeping multiple girlfriends happy under one very nice roof.

About the Author

Pilar Lastra may be best known for her suitcase-carrying skills on the popular NBC game show *Deal or No Deal*, but she is also the star of Playboy's hit web series *Hot Laps*. As the host of *Hot Laps*, Pilar test drives the coolest new cars, takes advanced car courses with the top driving instructors, rides laps with national champions, and shows her viewers her racing skills as a sponsored race car driver.

In addition to her work on *Deal or No Deal* and *Hot Laps*, Pilar has recurrently appeared on NBC's hit show *Las Vegas*, ESPN's *NFL News & Notes*, she emceed the *Miss Asia USA* Pageant, and starred in the cable hit comedy *Malibu Spring Break*. In 2006 she became the second playmate, alongside Jenny McCarthy, to be named one of *People* magazine's 100 Most Beautiful People. Pilar has appeared in several national print campaigns, such as Ford's Warriors in Pink, Jose Cuervo Black, and Wolverine Boots' *Mud Looks Good on Me* campaign, which graced the pages of Sports Illustrated Swimsuit Edition.

Pilar has also made a name for herself in radio, hosting several radio shows, including *The Playmate Hour, Mansion Mayhem*, and *The Playboy Fantasy Football Show* on Sirius/XM Fantasy Sports Channel. As a former host of *The Playmate Hour* on Sirius Satellite Radio, Pilar gave millions of listeners advice on love, sex, travel, and life through eyes of a playmate. Now as host of *Mansion Mayhem*, Pilar gives listeners a peek inside Hef's world of charity and the Playboy Mansion. *The Playboy Fantasy Football Show* has allowed Pilar to give her listeners inside tips directly from NFL stars to help win their Fantasy Football league. She was also a contributing writer to the novel "Naked Came the Summer," which was serialized on Sirius.com.

www.ingramcontent.com/pod-product-compliance
Lightning Source LLC
Chambersburg PA
CBHW020247290526
45784CB00003B/1135